Praise for Sherry Argov's Work

"A self-help classic."

—Daily Mail

"America's top relationship guide."

—The Book Tribe

One of "The 10 Most Iconic Relationship Books of the Past Ten Years."

—Yahoo!

"Men don't really go for 'nice.' They go for 'interesting.'"

—Chicago Sun-Times

"We're talking about having so much self-respect, Aretha Franklin would high-five you."

—Los Angeles Times

"The pejorative meaning of the word 'bitch' has been reclaimed . . . it means a strong, feisty woman who has moxie, and knows when to use it. A bitch is . . . sap free."

—Pursuit Magazine

"[Argov is] talking about a strong woman. Someone who knows what she's doing in life. Someone who will share the load, but who will stand her ground."

—Joy Behar, Co-host of *The View*

"Sherry Argov shows women how to transform a casual relationship into a committed one."

—The Today Show

"The Best of Culture."

—Esquire

Praise for Sherry Argov's Work

"A hot book!"

—*Fox News Channel*

"A must-read at Sunday brunch."

—*New York Daily News*

"*Why Men Love Bitches* flew off the shelves. . . . Men thrive with women who can set boundaries and who push back when they try to cross the line."

—*Cosmopolitan*

"An anti-whining manifesto that encourages women who feel like doormats to develop a sense of independence."

—*Playboy*

"Her sassy book is filled with scenarios and advice aimed at making women subtly stronger and self-empowered."

—*Publishers Weekly*

"If you've been too nice, run out and get this book now!"

—Ellen Fein and Sherrie Schneider,
authors of the *New York Times* Bestseller *The Rules*

WHY MEN MARRY *Bitches*

The Nice Woman's Guide to Getting *and Keeping* a Man's Heart

New York Times Bestselling Author
Sherry Argov

Avon, Massachusetts

First published in the UK in 2011 by Adams Media.

Adams Media is a division of F+W Media, Inc.
4700 East Galbraith Road
Cincinnati, OH 45236

This edition is for sale in the United Kingdom and Ireland only, not for export elsewhere.

A catalogue record for this book is available from the British Library.

ISBN-13: 978-0-7153-3768-4
ISBN-10: 0-7153-3768-8

Printed in Glasgow, Scotland by Thomson Litho Limited - Second Printing

For Mom, with love.

CONTENTS

6 BREAKING INTO THE *Boys Club*

7 FROM "I MIGHT" TO *"I Do"*

Acknowledgments

First and foremost, I thank and acknowledge my beautiful mother, Judy. Aside from being the best mother and my favorite person in the world, she taught me everything I know about how to be a strong woman, and how to see humor in everything. Making Mom proud is the only accomplishment that really matters.

I also want to thank the super teams at both Adams Media and F+W Media. I thank David Nussbaum, CEO and President of F+W Media. David Nussbaum is the kind of CEO someone is fortunate enough to work with once or twice in an entire career. I thank him for his special brand of leadership. I thank Chris Duffy, Royalties Manager at Adams Media, for being a consummate professional. I appreciate all the times he's gone the extra mile. I extend my gratitude to Sara Domville, President of the Book Division at F+W Media, and Karen Cooper, the Publisher of Adams Media. How cool it is to see two great women at the helm. I thank James Woollam,

Managing Director, for overseeing the release of this book, and Susie Hallam for handling publicity in the United Kingdom, Wales, Scotland, and Ireland. Thank you both for doing such a magnificent job! I offer special thanks to Stephanie McKenna, Foreign Rights Manager at Adams Media, who is the reason this book is selling in so many languages. I recognize Amy Collins, former Director of Sales at Adams Media, as the talented mind who originally led the book-launch efforts; she is my dear friend.

I want to thank Edward Colbert of Looney & Grossman, who is my brilliant lawyer, advisor, and counselor. I thank him for being in my corner, and for being someone I can *always* count on.

I want to thank my accountants, Kathryn Schmidt of Schmidt & Co., and Ali Adawiya of SongCare. They are both geniuses. I thank Dan Dydzak, lawyer and friend, for his friendship and pep talks at the local diner.

I want to thank Jeff Hyman, my photographer. His kindness will always be remembered. I thank Christine Serrao, of the Artist Relations department at MAC cosmetics, for her gracious help with my TV makeup.

I thank my special guy, who is my rock. (Fortunately for me, he doesn't read these kinds of books or take me too seriously.) Nevertheless, I thank him for his great suggestions on what I "really need to tell those bitches" after spending a day with "the guys."

I thank my favorite relatives who watch over me like angels: Tova, Samuel, Arnon, and Yossi Chait.

I thank my readers—my sisters—who tell all their girlfriends about my books, and who have taken the time to write me letters. I thank the good men out there who were kind enough to share how men think. The best part about writing a book such as this is meeting interesting people with a great sense of humor. I thank them for the privilege.

Introduction

Everyone's heard the story about the prince who marries the town maiden. Or the handsome eligible bachelor who could have any girl he wants, but who falls in love with an ordinary woman who is difficult to deal with. At the wedding, the guy feels like the luckiest guy in the world. Meanwhile, his family is popping antacids wondering, "Why her?" Then the speculation starts: "Is it the cooking? Is it the sex? Did she brainwash him? What did she do to him?" What they are dying to do is pull the guy aside and ask him point-blank, "Why are you marrying such a bitch?"

Why Men Marry Bitches is not another "how to fetch a husband" book. It's not a book that will even remotely suggest you are incomplete until you find your "better half." On the contrary. It will challenge convention, broaden your understanding of why some relationships don't progress, and modernize the way you think about how a man chooses his soul mate.

When I use the word *bitch*, the woman I'm describing is not cruel or mean. Throughout this book, as well as in my first release, *Why Men Love Bitches*, I use *bitch* in a tongue-in-cheek way. The term is intended to be satirical, and does not take itself too seriously. I use it to describe a strong woman who has her own identity and is secure with who she is. She is plenty happy giving him "space" because she enjoys having hers. She is clear about what she will or will not accept. She'll back away at the slightest whiff of disrespect, and this makes her more exciting to a man, not less. *That's the woman he dreams of marrying.*

We've all read Cinderella. We've seen the engagement ring commercials where the woman gets her glistening bling bling. We've been at weddings in which there are ten bridesmaids dressed like Tinkerbell. Then the photographer takes a picture of all the bridesmaids surrounding the bride, crouching over her left hand and staring adoringly at the big rock. Then comes the toss of the bouquet, and all the single women trample over one another to catch it, so that somebody's prepubescent nephew wearing braces can put a garter on her thigh. That's how women respond to the *very idea* of being married.

Men observe this. They watch women act like marriage is the be all and end all and they make a mental note. It only confirms what he's always known: Marriage doesn't necessarily mean she's in love with him. Some men feel that the woman is in love with *the wedding* or *what marriage represents.* He's just there to fill a position.

All of this influences how men date. They avoid situations in which they suspect a woman needs a relationship to feel whole, because there again, he feels he's just filling a position. For a man, a needy woman equals entrapment because she doesn't love him for who he is. The truth is that men aren't commitment phobic, *they want love and marriage just as much as women do.*

In order for a man to desire marriage, he has to think, "Gee that would be a wonderful thing to be married to her." And that doesn't happen when a woman follows the conventional advice and forces the issue: "I need to know where this is going. I don't want to waste my time." These are things women say automatically. A woman will think she's saving time, but what she doesn't realize is that she's just talked him out of it. When a woman acts like a relationship, a commitment, or a marriage is "owed" to her, she will send him running in the other direction.

That's why this book was written.

In the chapters you are about to read, you will learn to alter your approach. You will understand why he needs to wonder why you *aren't* behaving as though you are desperate to be married like every other woman he meets. When you seem different in that you aren't coming at him with a "marry me" agenda, that's when you'll get more proposals than you'll know what to do with.

You'll also understand how men *really* think. What their actions *really* mean. How he *expects* you to react, and how you *should* behave instead. And not the same old "fluff" you've read in other relationship books. You will learn all the things that men know, and bitches know . . . but that nice girls have yet to learn.

The material in my books is drawn less from my opinion and more from the information I gathered from hundreds of hours of interviews with men who sat down and talked with me candidly. They gave me an inside look at the information usually reserved for men only, about what really gets a man to fall in love and pop the question.

It was so important to me to be accurate that I even reread the material to men before it went to press to ensure that it accurately reflected how they feel. They would say, "If women had these traits, we'd be much more willing to get married. I'm so glad you are telling this to women. Just don't use my real name . . . ."

After the release of my first book, I heard a lot of critics say, "Women should never play games." From where I sit, this is very amusing because it implies that men are always compassionate, altruistic, and honest—and in no way playing games with women. The reality is that men stretch the truth and strategically omit critical information all the time in order to have their cake and eat it too. In the same way that a pretty woman uses her looks to get perks and benefits, men hint at the possibility of "marriage someday" to string women along.

The following chapters will teach you why doting on a man to show "how much you care" is often the very behavior that leads him to decide you aren't interesting enough to pursue. Bending over backward does not bring you the love and attention you crave. But having your own life, your own goals, and a backbone will.

That doesn't mean this book is only for women who want to walk down the aisle. Perhaps you are married and want to spice things up. You may want to stay single. This book is about how to *capture his heart* so you have the power to choose the outcome *you* want.

So take off your rose-colored glasses and throw them out the window. It's time to start asking whether he's really good enough *for you*. You will come to acquire that special X factor so you can feel like you are always at the controls. And you will learn how to make him feel you are the special one he *can't live without*.

Go grab a glass of wine, or a cup of tea. Take your shoes off and put your feet up, because we are going to do some *serious* girl talking here. And fair warning, people: This is no "coddle your inner child" book.

Note: Throughout this book, names of men and women have been changed to protect the not-so-innocent.

1

THROWING OUT THE *Rulebook*

Why a Strong Woman Wins His Heart

Let us now set forth one of the fundamental truths about marriage: the wife is in charge.

~BILL COSBY

Society's Guidelines for Good Girls

Imagine a world in which roles were reversed and men cooked for women, picked up socks, and couldn't wait to get married. Pretend you had a boyfriend who owned a hope chest with six lavender bow ties inside that he wanted his groomsmen to wear at the wedding. Picture him getting choked up every time you strolled past a Baby Gap. And that he greeted you at the door wearing silk boxers and cowboy boots, so he could do a pole dance for you. Then add a few ultimatums:

"Where's my ring?"

"Why won't you marry me?"

Chances are, you would assume the guy wasn't firing on all cylinders. And then you'd start planning your escape. "It's not you, it's me. [Translation: It's definitely you.] I'm too busy with work. I love you but I'm not in love with you." Then you'd blow out the door . . . like TNT.

As scary as it sounds, this is precisely the approach women are taught on how to catch a husband. It's the plight of every "nice girl" who puts everyone else first, puts her own needs last, and doesn't think she is worthy of touching the hemline of her man's pants.

When I polled men, they all said *confident women are in very short supply.* And that a confident woman is what they find sexiest. Is it any wonder that confident women are hard to come by? Look around. The average fashion magazine tells women to act like a servant, as if dating were a labor-intensive, blue-collar-job application: "Can you serve a cold beer in trashy lingerie? Do you leave razor-sharp creases in his shirts like employee-of-the-month at the Jolly Roger motel? Do you wear cellophane for him? Are you gardening in stilettos? Are you giving it up doggie-style? If so, he'll drop to one knee and propose . . . ."

What women are learning from all of this is how to behave desperately. When her attitude is "Pick me! Pick me!" she hits the kill switch on his desire. It's human nature. You'd be just as turned off by a guy who brought two dozen roses to a first coffee date and told you he felt like the luckiest SOB on the planet in the first five minutes.

It's human nature. Telling a woman to work harder to please is like telling a little kid to walk up to a schoolyard bully on the first day of school and say, "Here, take my lunch money. And you can have my cupcakes too. I'll even throw in my lunchbox since you don't have one." Or, in a dating situation, "Here, take my body. And I made you a cake. Please be nice. Please marry me. I'll even jack my butt up nice and high like they do in yoga. It's so comfortable being upside down. *Really*. I just love it!"

Just because a man sleeps with you doesn't mean he's thinking about the future. For him to think about forever, there has to be something he respects *within* you. Like a strong wit . . . and a strong mind.

RELATIONSHIP PRINCIPLE 1

In romance, there's nothing more attractive to a man than a woman who has dignity and pride in who she is.

In addition, you have to know your own mind. The more you focus on elevating yourself, the more he will work to be at the top of your priority list. He considers you a long-term prospect when you've added the key ingredient: *respect*. And respect is the glue that holds everything together.

Kara is a perfect example of why smart, confident women come out on top. Very early on, her fiance tried to give her his two cents on how she should dress. She was leaving for a meeting, and he told her to wear a dress instead of the pantsuit she had on. Then he told her she was wearing too much makeup. What the nice girl would have done is run out and buy a new wardrobe. But Kara playfully put him in check: "Listen here, Versace. This outfit has always been fine. And I haven't had any complaints about the makeup either. But if you'd like, I'll let you know when I'm wearing this in advance. That way, if you don't want to see me in it, you don't have to come over."

In order to be looked at differently, you have to *think* differently. He has to see that you call your own shots and that you don't need input from anyone about how to put your socks on. This says, "I am secure." The biggest attraction killer is neediness and insecurity. The bitch doesn't audition or try to be the "best in show." Instead of "where's my ring" or "why won't you marry me," she's thinking:

"What's the advantage of having this guy around?"

"How do I feel about myself after I've been in his company?"

"What's in it for me?"

And then a funny thing happens: *He falls all over himself* to be with her.

Kim Basinger said something interesting: "I don't have time to be classified as difficult, and I don't have time to care." Men tend to feel at ease with a woman who doesn't care so much because then he doesn't have to be fully responsible for someone else's happiness. When a man sees you are happy with him *but you can be just as happy having nothing to do with him*, that's when he won't want to leave your side. *When you are happy, you are sexy.*

Not only this, bitches have more fun. My friend Angela had a date with a guy on a Friday and they went out for Chinese food. They tried several dishes and had plenty of leftovers, so Angela took home all the doggie bags. The following evening, she had date with a different guy and decided to be the "hostess with the mostest." She reheated the Chinese leftovers, "reorganized" a medley on a pretty plate, and served it to her guest of honor. The fortune cookie said: "The catered din-din was a smashing success."

Of course, I would never recommend that you choose such a quick and easy meal over three hours of sweating and slaving in the kitchen. However, I would be remiss if I did not include this one expert gourmet cooking tip: Don't keep the parsley. (If it gets soggy in the microwave it will be a dead giveaway every time.)

Notice what Kara and Angela had in common: Neither one of them felt the need to overcompensate. This earned the man's respect. Why? It was *expected* that they knock themselves out because the rulebook says women are supposed to. When they refused, a light bulb went off over his head. The message "I am worth something" *is what turns him into a believer.*

In a music-channel documentary, Tim McGraw said something very intriguing about his wife, Faith Hill: "She's a straight shooter, that's for sure. She doesn't take any sh★t from anybody." He didn't choose to comment on her talent, success, beauty, fame, or any of the other things society celebrates. Instead, he commented on the attribute men respect most: a backbone. Do you think he's proud that his wife doesn't take B.S. lying down? I'd bet that he is.

RELATIONSHIP PRINCIPLE 2

He marries the woman who *won't* lay down like linoleum.

This brings us to the definition of a marrying bitch—aka a strong, spirited woman who can stand up for herself. The bitch is not rude or abrasive because she's smart enough to know that being considerate is more effective. But she won't compromise herself to be in a relationship. She won't work overtime to "catch a husband." Because of this, he doesn't classify her as a mindless woman he can take advantage of. She has a certain moxie about her. Sugar and spice . . . and *not* always so nice—*that's what his dreams are made of.*

Since many "nice" women mistakenly believe that being a strong woman (aka a bitch) is a bad thing, let's explore some of the criteria of the so-called eligible woman. Then we'll find out from men what they *really* think about women who behave this way.

Myth 1: You Have to Be Perfect

Think about the last time you were madly in love. Chances are, the guy wasn't a millionaire or a brain surgeon with six-pack abs who was hung like a barnyard animal on Viagra. Chances are, he didn't get you off five times before he got his. But there was something special about him. He had a couple of features that did it for you and a certain magic that made you tingle. Men who want to fit in a relationship are looking for that same magic.

RELATIONSHIP PRINCIPLE 3

He doesn't marry a woman who is perfect. He marries the woman who is *interesting*.

This is one of the biggest myths perpetuated by the media: If you are perfect, beautiful, and rich, you will get the respect and love you crave. So they say. (And now back to reality.) When a man meets a woman who seems *too* perfect, *too* sweet, or *too* agreeable, he tends to become bored very quickly.

Beauty pageants are a good example of how women are misled into thinking that the most important pursuits in life are beauty tips and "man catching" skills. Granted, they offer educational grants and scholarships, which is very ironic because the only men watching are the ones who like really stupid women. Intelligent men think it's embarrassing for a woman to pose and smile like she's always that chipper. Everybody knows the losers want to strangle the winner, and the Southern Belle who wins Miss Congeniality is dying to tell the judges: "Fuck all, y'all . . . you ugly summabitches." All of them pretend to be virgins until marriage, and all are do-gooders for the poor:

SECOND RUNNER-UP:

"I am a fifth-year junior at the local college majoring in pottery. I plan to end world hunger and find a cure for cancer. And once and for all, I intend to put an end to the global shortage of flower pots."

FIRST RUNNER-UP:

"I plan to feed the starving, the homeless, the unemployed, and the destitute. That way all my relatives can eat."

QUEEN BEE:

"Before I visit poverty-stricken villages in Africa, I'm fixin' to get my toes painted. Invite the press. I'm wearing my thousand-dollar Manolo Blahnik shoes!"

If you've ever noticed, beauty pageants are a lot like county fairs. The farmers show the cows the same way. They walk their prized Jersey cow across a stage in front of an audience with judges, and maybe the cow even twirls around a couple of times. Then the winning cow gets a satin ribbon draped over it, which has the title and the year on it. They even have twelve-month calendars featuring the "cow of the month."

So let's try to apply this Barbie-like behavior to a first date to see why it goes over like a lead balloon. Picture a woman trying to be that "perfect girl." She walks into the room like she's on a catwalk. The handbag matches the shoe button. She giggles on cue. For dinner, she orders two olives with low-cal dressing (on the side). Without realizing it, this woman has already marked herself: *temporary*. In his mind? "Deposit and go." He may have sex with her, but from there on it's a downhill slide. Why?

When she's artificial, he becomes wary of who she really is and what her real motivations are. Usually, he figures she's putting on a show to trap him. So it never goes to the next level. This is why some relationships never shift into second gear. By trying to be something she's not, the woman automatically gets marked with the "insecure" stamp. "This one will need constant attention and nothing I give will ever be enough. She'll sap me of all my energy." Before he's spent any time with her, he is mentally on to the next.

Not only this, but when a man thinks a woman is weak or insecure, he won't feel the need to work at the relationship. It becomes "male entertainment" at that point. The relationship becomes a sideshow. He'll kick back, crack a beer, and think, "She's trying so hard, I'll never have to break a sweat in this relationship."

RELATIONSHIP PRINCIPLE 4

When a woman is trying too hard, a man will usually test to see how hard she's willing to work for it. He'll start throwing relationship Frisbees, just to see how hard she'll run and how high she'll jump.

Men are *used* to this. So they try to bait you into this behavior. He may tell you on a second date that he likes red toenail polish. Or that he likes a particular item of clothing. If you immediately begin to "work" to be what he wants, it lessens his respect.

To better understand, let's take a sneak peek at a page inside the *male* rulebook. This is the hush-hush highly classified stuff.

A PAGE FROM THE MALE RULEBOOK

The definition of unforgettably sexy: A woman who can function on her own and take care of herself. She won't let me always have the upper hand. And, she can tell anyone to go jump in the lake whenever she feels like it.

That's the woman he'll work harder to be with. Whenever you are too worried about someone else's approval, *that person loses respect for you.* When a man sees you knocking yourself out from the jump start, you are setting yourself up for a lopsided relationship, because you reinforce every guy's unspoken belief: "If you ignore her, she'll seek your validation and reassurance." Approval then becomes his only "contribution." *When you need his approval, it blinds you* and you quickly become the vulnerable one in the relationship. Adopt the philosophy of "approval neither desired nor required."

After all, there will always be someone there to tell you that you aren't attractive enough, perfect enough, or that you didn't come from the right side of the tracks. True confidence is born when you . . .

RELATIONSHIP PRINCIPLE 5

Don't believe what anyone tells you about yourself.

Sophia Loren said, "Beauty is how you feel inside, and it reflects in your eyes. It is not something physical." This is what makes you gorgeous to a quality man, because now you arrive complete. And that makes him say, "Gee, I wonder, what is that special magic she's got?"

How does this affect long-term relationships? When a man can't crack your code, or figure out where your insecurities are, *you are no longer readable*. That's when he doesn't have a 100 percent hold on you, and he has to put in his 50 percent share to win you over, keep your interest, and maintain a reciprocal and viable relationship.

Myth 2: You Have to Be His Sex Toy

Men love to tell colorful stories that sound just like the ones they read in men's magazines. According to him, all his ex-girlfriends are supermodels and had sex with him ten times a day. Clearly, a figment of his imagination. To prove it, all you have to do is take a quick look at a photo of his ex-girlfriend. If it is true she gave it up ten times a day, there will be visible signs. The back of her head will look like a rat's nest. Her ankles will be permanently affixed behind her ears. And she'll be so emaciated, someone will be tossing her a cheeseburger.

Women also get confused about what men want from observing the magazines men read. For example, nudie magazines. I don't know about you, but I don't regularly sit on a bale of hay in the middle a cornfield, butt naked, in order to catch a sunset. No matter how freezing it is, the model is usually sucking on a finger while hanging upside down from a tree, and is quoted as saying, "I love being naked. It makes me feel so close to nature." Then comes the first-rate literature.

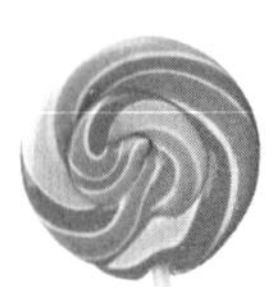

Turn-ons: Twinkies, Popsicles, and sunsets.

Most influential person in my life: My puppy.

Favorite sport: Naked kayaking.

Proudest accomplishment: Tying both shoelaces in under five minutes.

Naturally, women see these formidable influences and think, "This is how I have to behave. If I am a freak in the bedroom, and I cook a mean meat loaf, he'll run out and buy me a ring. Right?" Doubtful. When a man comes home from a hard day's work, the last thing he wants is to find his wife naked on the front porch, licking a multicolored lollipop, wearing her hair in pigtails, and watering the tulips. He'll be thinking, "She's two sandwiches short of a picnic."

I asked one guy if this is what men fantasize about. He wanted to answer my question but couldn't stop laughing. Then he said, "Definitely a turn-off. She's not really being herself."

A smart, together guy won't build a life with a woman he feels doesn't have her feet firmly planted on the ground. Men do not marry the "little girl" types because they don't want to feel like they are adopting a young child. The only reason men like stupid women is so they can take advantage of them—in the short term. A quality guy worth his salt wants a partner who is competent and multidimensional. Someone who can handle things when he's not around.

That doesn't mean men won't break their necks to *look* at a woman who is showing a lot of skin. But at the same time, they'll pass judgment: "Short-term only." And once a man categorizes you as "sex only," he won't see anything beyond that.

RELATIONSHIP PRINCIPLE 6

Men see how you dress, and then make assumptions about your relationship potential.

A man named Doug explained, "It makes a woman *more* attractive if she's showing *less* skin. It makes you want to find out what's underneath. A guy doesn't want to get to bed and think, 'No big deal. I've already seen this.' You want her birthday suit to be a surprise. That's half the excitement."

When women look at clothing, we see colors, fabrics, and styles. What do men see? Whether or not you are a mental challenge. That's why you hear men talk about nurse fantasies or the girl-next-door or librarian types. If a woman wears something that doesn't "show all her stuff," like jeans and a sweater, what a guy reads is: "It's not here on display for you. *You'll have to work a little to get this.*" When a woman shows a little but not all, a guy infers that the sexy parts of her are "privileged" areas. And her stock goes up.

Evan is a classic example of how quickly men categorize women. He met Blair at work and asked her if she'd like to have drinks that evening. She was wearing a silk blouse that showed a little, but not too much. Then she ran home to freshen up. Thinking she was going to "wow" him, she put on a cropped T-shirt that showed tons of cleavage and a belly ring, with large lettering across her chest that read NOT EVERYTHING IS FLAT IN KANSAS. He recalls, "I knew it wasn't going anywhere from day one."

If he wants a serious relationship with a woman, he'd rather see less skin in public and keep the freak show private, for his eyes only. He'd rather see a formfitting blouse than a plunging neckline. Or a sundress that shows a hint of her silhouette. He's much more fascinated by a long skirt with a slit up the side than a micro-mini that shows the whole leg. Why? The peek-a-boo element. Not knowing when her leg will pop out triggers his imagination. And once you get him curious and *thinking about you*, that's when his thoughts turn to the future.

RELATIONSHIP PRINCIPLE 7

When a man sees you wearing very revealing clothes, he'll usually assume you don't have anything else going for you.

Once he reduces you to one dimension, he'll keep you there. He'll never take you seriously or think of you as having enough worth for a long-term relationship. Men want to marry a woman who is the whole package. News flash: If men were to explain this to women, they'd never get laid.

According to the media, it's *hip* for you to invite a girlfriend over and have a ménage à trois. And it's *cool* to break out the naughty-schoolgirl outfit or jump up and down on a pole wearing a wig and a Little Bo Peep costume. Some fitness centers even have classes that teach women how to dance like a stripper. Women begin grinding their chairs and crawling across the floor on their hands and knees while "Ain't Too Proud To Beg" is blaring over the loudspeaker.

While it might be really comical to watch as you look on from the treadmill, you can't be thinking, "Uh-oh. I better give him a lap dance in the La-Z-Boy to keep him happy." (Slap yourself, before I do it for you.) If you use sex to catch him, you will be guaranteed immediate contact and he'll put you in his little black book. But you won't get the rice . . . the ring . . . and the nonstick cooking set.

Whom would you see a long-term future with? A Chippendale's dancer wearing a neon-yellow thong with singles inside his jockstrap, and plenty of wiggle in his jiggle? Or a nice-looking guy in a three-piece suit, with a 401(k)? Likewise, men want the whole package. They fantasize about having a quality woman they are proud of, whom they'd cuddle up with next to a fireplace. Another news flash: A quality guy won't marry a woman who *cheapens* herself.

Have you ever noticed that even strippers don't like the word *stripper*? Oops. Excuse me for being so insensitive. I respectfully confirm they are indeed "exotic dancers" earning an honorable living while paying their way through medical school. And my neighborhood crack dealer is an exotic pharmacist. As soon as he finishes his undergrad in the chemical arts, he is pursuing a doctorate in pharmacology.

Remember, if you show up wearing a rhinestone thong pulled up to your hips on the first date, and on the next date you're sporting a miniskirt that could double as a tube top from the children's department, he'll see you as community property: "Any guy can get to it so I'm not special if I can get to her."

Not only this, but men are extremely insecure about how many other lovers you've had, *especially* if they're thinking about marriage. Men even admitted that they have a magic number in their heads when they ask how many men you've been with. (Anything more than what can be counted on one hand is too many.) And it takes very little for their imaginations to run wild.

If you see him in an old pair of underwear that has a large hole next to little lefty, you assume he hasn't had a good woman in his life to buy him a new supply of "tighty whities." With men it's the opposite. If he sees you wearing a sexy panty but the elastic is a little frayed or tattered, he'll see it as evidence of a recent humping. The same goes for that black lacy see-through bra you were planning to wear for him. If it's missing a hook or the hook is bent sideways (heaven forbid), he'll think it's been violently snatched off your body a time or two.

RELATIONSHIP PRINCIPLE 8

When he sees you scantily dressed, he is not reminded of how great you look naked. He immediately thinks of all the other men you've slept with.

For this reason, hold fire on the five-piece triple XXX crotch-less outfit with fishnets, rubber, metal studs, and fifteen straps. It will have an "everybody's girlfriend" feel to it. What most men said they find sexiest is a woman in one of his shirts with a sexy pair of panties underneath. This has a "mine only" feel. If you change into sleepwear, wear something silky that looks like you'd wear it for yourself when he's not around. This is more likely to make him appreciate the sex, and appreciate you also.

Stated or not, most guys want to feel like Farmer John plowing new turf. (And your job is to keep that illusion going.)

Myth 3: You Have to Be Whatever He Wants You to Be

This is one of the key differences between a bitch and a nice girl. The nice girl meets a guy and acts like she joined a cult. If he's a Grape-Nuts and berry-eating spiritual type, she's eating berries with her morning chants. If he's Italian, she's making meatballs. If he's Jewish, she's rolling up matzo balls. If he's a fan of boating, she subscribes to *Power Boat* magazine. If he's an environmentalist, she's hugging trees, sucking down wheat grass, and trading in her SUV for a hybrid.

This is why when you see a man who is madly in love with his wife, usually she's a woman with a mind of her own. She doesn't "suffer fools gladly." The lights are on . . . and the bitch is home.

When Michael J. Fox met his wife, Tracy Pollan, they were taping an episode of *Family Ties*. On a lunch break, he walked over to her and made a rude remark about her breath. "Man, did you have the scampi for lunch or what?" She immediately told him off and walked away. To this day he recalls, "I had a crush on her from that point on."

If Michael J. Fox is like most guys, what impressed him is that his wife wasn't a pushover. She checked him like a sweaty hockey player when he stepped over the line. *And he liked it.* They're married with four kids, and twenty years later he still talks about how beautiful he thinks she is in TV interviews.

Self-respect is a one-punch knockout to a guy. When you are confident enough to wield your power and you show that you aren't fearful of losing him, he becomes fearful of losing you. "Wow. She's quick. This one is quality. I will need to mind my p's and q's to show her my *finer* qualities in order to keep her interest." And just like that—Domino's pizza and beer will be upgraded to red roses and Cristal champagne.

Case in point. Roger and Cheryl are as different as night and day. He likes the finer things in life. Cheryl loves the 99 Cent Store, a place where he wouldn't be caught dead. (He says, "That's where peasants shop.") When she goes into thrift stores, he waits in the car, ducking behind the wheel to avoid being recognized. But that doesn't keep

Cheryl from going. She'll make a sandwich for Roger, and after he eats it she'll harass him: "Pretty good, huh? And all the ingredients came from the 99 Cent Store." The man adores her so much, he'd lie down in traffic for her.

When a man likes you, he will be interested in finding out what you like. If he makes you happy, he feels more secure. Everything men do is intended to impress women—whether it's going to the moon, becoming a rock star, or driving a nice car. The Taj Mahal was built for a woman. The toys, the homes, the power suits . . . it's all designed to impress a woman. *Be that woman.*

When he asks what kind of food you like, be honest. It's a good thing for you to tell him how to please you because *pleasing you keeps him engaged in the relationship.*

In the beginning, a guy might ask a woman what she likes. The nice girl makes the mistake of shrugging her shoulders. "I like anything you like. Whatever . . . I'm easy." She thinks she's being considerate, but what she's getting across is, "I'll take you any way I can have you . . . even if you give me crumbs."

So let's dispel a couple of nice-girl myths.

1. To a guy, a "whatever girl" is the same as a "yes girl."

A classic example: Picture a guy taking you to a bad movie and then asking what you thought of the movie. If it's horrible and you say, "Great special effects!" he'll respect you a little less than if you say, "Good company, but the movie sucked. And here's why I thought it wasn't that good. . . ." When a man can depend on you to shoot straight and speak your mind, he will view you as a more legitimate candidate.

What men read from the "whatever" or "okeydoke" agreeable woman type is: "I'm not confident enough to make decisions." This is one of the ways men evaluate whether you are "relationship material" and "marriage material." He doesn't marry a Stepford Wife or clinker-top toy that nods its head with every movement. This brings us to the second nice-girl lesson:

2. The fastest way to become boring to a man is to always "do as you are told."

There were many times I interviewed married men who specifically said this attribute would make or break the relationship. One married man said, "There were a few women I dated but couldn't bring myself to marry. They were always the women who were willing to drop everything and do anything I wanted."

RELATIONSHIP PRINCIPLE 9

Every guy knows he can find a girl who is simply satisfied with satisfying *him*. They are much more turned on by a woman who cares about her own pleasure as well.

What a quality guy secretly longs for is a lover who is also a best friend. And an equal partner. When I interviewed men, I was always stunned when they talked about "an emotional connection." One of them surprised me when he said, "A man wants all the things a woman wants. If you really care about her, you'll wonder what kind of wife she'd be. But most men don't admit that because they don't want the woman knowing he cares *that* much. It's safer to express sexual interest only, because it's still considered 'manly' But deep down, men want an emotional connection as well."

Not only this, but being too agreeable prevents you from learning key things about him before you commit to a long-term relationship. One of the key things you want to learn about a man is how much he *respects your opinion.*

RELATIONSHIP PRINCIPLE 10

You can tell how much someone respects you by how much he respects your opinion. If he doesn't respect your opinion, *he won't respect you.*

When you "go along to get along" or are too agreeable and passive, you invite his disrespect.

Cynthia was on a date and Jon asked, "What do you do for fun?" Cynthia responded, "I bought a high-end riding lawn mower. Last weekend I had fun mowing my front lawn." Then she described a few other hobbies. Here's what he observed: "She didn't care that I might think it's stupid or quirky. That is her thing and that's who she is. The fact that she was proud of it was a complete turn-on."

He didn't have to like it. But he respected it. This is why you hear happily married couples say, "We really adore each other . . . even though we have nothing in common."

Whenever someone is telling you to be *different* than who you are, they are stifling you. There's a kind of bondage that comes with being in the mainstream.

Think of the classic scene from *American Beauty*. At the end of the movie Angela, the pretty, blond cheerleader, gets into an altercation with her dowdy girlfriend Jane. At one point, Angela says to Jane, "At least I'm not ugly!" Jane's boyfriend says to Angela, "Yes you are. And you are boring. And you are totally ordinary, and you know it."

This is the exact opposite of what women are taught. Some women aren't lucky enough to have a parent, teacher, or other role model who tells her to develop a skill set, a career, or to believe in herself. The unspoken message is that women should invest in their man-catching skills instead. "Someday a man will come along and take care of you." Does he? Yes. He rolls out the red carpet when *you don't need him to*. In other words, when you act like you're associating with him because he's cute and you have some free time to kill. Not because he's the "end all" of end alls.

Men pick up on how much you need them *and they instantly feel pressured and back off.* The pressure is lifted when you become passionate about your life, don't give yourself away, and stay focused on pursuing your dreams.

Men used different words, but overwhelmingly they all said the same thing. The pressure becomes unbearable for a man when a woman is overrun by obsession with the relationship, when her whole worldview boils down to him. "What if he does X. Should I do Y? What if he says this? . . . Should I say that?" Men assume the woman is sprung or obsessed when she stops giving her opinion and becomes afraid to say, "No, I don't want to do that." Or, "No, I won't go there." The end result? A crash landing.

Ever wondered why men are intrigued by redheads? It's because they're different. Men like anything different, that everyone else doesn't have.

RELATIONSHIP PRINCIPLE 11

It is better to be disliked for being *who you are* than to be loved for *who you are not.*

In the movie *Closer*, Natalie Portman asks Jude Law why he is so madly in love with the photographer, played by Julia Roberts. "Is it because she's successful?" Jude Law quips, "No. It's because *she doesn't need me.*"

To better understand why it turns a man on to feel like you are a "cat of a different breed," let's refer to another page from the secret male rulebook:

A PAGE FROM THE MALE RULEBOOK

It's a man's world so we are used to getting our way. But when a woman has her own way of doing things, she becomes very intriguing. Even though we seem a little confused when we don't get our way, we secretly respect it. Suddenly, we get to see things from a different perspective. And then we spend the rest of our time trying to figure out how we can fit into *her* spicy world.

Now, let's talk about how to introduce him into . . . your spicy world.

2

MAKE HIM CHASE *You* UNTIL YOU CATCH *Him*

How to Convince Him Commitment Was *His* Idea

When women go wrong, men go right after them.

~MAE WEST

The Bitch Gets Him to Drop His Guard

You can't wrestle a man down like a wrangler at the rodeo and hog-tie him to get a commitment. Just like the little calf, he'll run like hell to get away from you. Instead of trying to lasso or hook a guy, you have to change your approach. When it comes to commitment, *he hooks himself.* All you have to do is be feminine, soft, charming, and enjoyable to be around. Then toss *him* the rope. Watch. He'll get all tangled up in it.

Deep down, men want to be chivalrous. They want to have a woman they can cherish and do everything for. Just like a woman's instinct is to please, a man's instinct is to pursue. He wants you to think he is dark, smoky, and mysterious like James Dean in *Rebel Without a Cause*. He wants to feel he's blindsiding you with his "mojo" spell and you are taken by him. But wait . . . not *too* easily taken. He wants to win you over . . . *incrementally*.

RELATIONSHIP PRINCIPLE 12

Men like to be curious.

They like to feel that there's more to

the story than what they already know.

Mandy is a perfect example of a woman who tried to accelerate this process. Brandon wanted to take her to dinner on a second date, but she insisted on cooking instead. When he came over, he encountered a five-star production. She served foie gras, the finest goose-liver pate in the world. When he reached for the salt, she started apologizing. "My cooking is usually better than this." What she divulged is that she cares too much . . . and too soon.

Here's Brandon's take: "After foie gras, I know I'm getting laid. And I know she wants a ring on her finger. But if she throws me a sandwich or a sloppy joe, that means I still have something to prove. When I'm not quite sure *how much* she likes me, that's when the challenge is on."

If you let on that you are insecure about winning him over, he will know he has you. And if he knows he has you, it's unlikely you will engender that overwhelming feeling of attraction that is necessary for him to want to marry you. Once it's obvious you are *totally* 100 percent hooked, there's nothing exciting about you anymore.

RELATIONSHIP PRINCIPLE 13

The mental challenge is not, "Can I get her to sleep with me?" The mental challenge is, "Can I get *and keep* her attention?"

A man taking on a new relationship is like a young boy opening a new jigsaw puzzle for the very first time. If he opens up the box and the puzzle is already put together, all the fun and excitement is taken out of it. But if the kid has to think, imagine, strategize, and put all the little pieces together, his mind is being stimulated. And then the little boy is tickled pink.

When it comes to securing a man's interest in commitment, your best strategy is to behave as if you like him, but you *aren't* that interested in locking him down. The objective is not to be standoffish, just low key. The lower the profile, the more he'll come in for the kill. And by "low profile" I mean, appear happy to see him, just don't *assume the role of his girlfriend*. When you don't step into that role, he'll lower his guard and begin to pursue *you*.

The reason for this is that men are programmed to protect their freedom. He starts off halfway suspicious that you want to get married to begin with. So the minute you start talking about commitment, hinting about marriage, or appearing to want to take him down, he'll "do battle" to fight for his freedom. The second you utter words like *monogamy*, *kids*, or *minivan*, he'll put up a wall. In his mind, every woman is looking for a "live one" so she can plot his capture . . . arrest . . . and future life in captivity.

Ever wondered why men read women's magazines? They're spying on the opposition. A man will read all the articles like "How to Get Him to Commit Even Though He Slept with Your Little Sister and Cousin with Buck Teeth." They always show a picture of a guy with his back turned to a pouty-looking woman wearing a ninety-dollar bra. So he figures, "All women have a preset agenda."

What makes matters even worse is all the horrible advice about how a woman should verbally "negotiate" a relationship. Whether it's exclusivity in the beginning or getting engaged a year later, the conventional wisdom is to put your cards on the table and tell him you want a relationship (as if he doesn't already know). In other words, get busy on the fast track. This, the so-called experts say, will save time and cut to the chase so you can know going in whether or not he's "marriage minded." Right? Not so fast.

Men have a name for this. They call it "the talk." It's the first sign of trouble. Here are some of the things women say during dinner conversation or pillow talk within the first couple of months:

The Dreaded "Talk"

- Where is this headed?
- What do you see in the future?
- How do you feel about commitment?
- I'm looking for the one.
- Do you want to settle down?
- I refuse to waste my time in a dead-end situation.
- I'd like to have children.
- Do you ever see yourself getting married? Or remarried?
- I am looking for security. What are you looking for?
- My clock is ticking.

The woman thinks she's subtly beating around the bush, or helping to move things along. But to a guy? He sees this as *way too obvious*. It's as blatant as a farmer opening up the mouth of a work mule to examine the teeth: "Good stock! I'll take him."

RELATIONSHIP PRINCIPLE 14

Your power gets lost the minute you start asking, "Where do I stand?" Because what you've just told him is that the terms of the relationship are now *his to dictate*.

If it happens too soon, he will usually feel he's being coerced into a plan that is no longer his. Even one or two of the above questions and . . . *poof*!

- Alarms will go off,
- His guard will go up, and
- He'll start planning his escape
- He just won't show it (until after he sleeps with you)

He may stick around for three months, or he may exit after six. But if you've told him you won't "waste your time in a dead-end relationship" or that you want to be married within one year, all you've done is tell him you're someone he needs to get away from. This is why being up front and "open" doesn't work.

RELATIONSHIP PRINCIPLE 15

As soon as a man has his guard up,
he will not fall in love or get attached.

The only way he'll get attached is if
you lower his guard first.

It's a little like a woman's approach to sex. If a guy hits on you in a bar and comes on too strong, chances are you'll think, "It's hardly a compliment. He's so horny, he'll shack up with anything in a skirt." Because the guy is being so obvious, your guard immediately goes up and you want nothing more to do with him. Right?

This is exactly how men approach commitment and marriage. They feel like most women would marry a toothless ex-convict as long as he got on bended knee and told her she had a pretty hairdo. So, the second you bring it up, or you seem too fixated on securing a serious relationship from the jump start, you get categorized as having "a plan" or "an agenda." And then *his interest in anything long term will go right out the window.*

RELATIONSHIP PRINCIPLE 16

When a woman rushes in too quickly, a man will assume she is in love with a "fantasy" or the *idea* of having a relationship. But if he has to slowly win her over, incrementally, he'll think she's falling in love with *who he is*.

To him, a vacant "boyfriend slot" or an open "husband position" looks about as desirable as stepping into an open bear trap. He wants to feel like he won a special girl who isn't easily obtained. And no guy feels that way if she comes across as having an opening that was available before he even got there.

Eddie explained, "My ex-girlfriend told me, 'Most men would jump at the chance to marry me. And if you don't marry me, I might end up marrying one of your friends.' That's like a guy saying to a woman, 'If you don't bang me, I'll get one of your girlfriends to do it.' Women say that stuff about marriage all the time and have no idea how it comes across."

In his mind, you are cheapening the relationship. You want a husband quickly, but you don't necessarily want quality. That makes him feel like an ordinary chump. And everyone wants to feel like they are special.

Also, joking won't make your motives any less obvious. Allison is a perfect example. She and Jamie had been out a few times, and one night they had a few too many drinks. She looked at him and jokingly said, "Am I just a piece of ass, or do you have feelings for me?" What this says to a guy is that she has low self-esteem. If she knows she's not a piece of booty, she would never ask that question.

So rule number one: You have to be coy. You have to come at him in a *different* way than what he's used to encountering.

RELATIONSHIP PRINCIPLE 17

Don't even mention the word "commitment."

That's the whole trick.

The less you say about it,

the closer you are to getting one.

In fact, each time you say *commitment* you've just added on a few weeks or months. And don't talk about exclusivity or monogamy. The less you ask, the more he'll tell. All negotiations should be 95 percent non-verbal and 5 percent verbal. You have to act like you are still getting to know him, and that commitment is nowhere on your radar.

This will disarm him. Now he's a warrior without a battle plan because has no idea how to swing his ax. With the nice girl, he can see what her plan is and win. But with a bitch, he *can't* see his opponent or her plan. This is precisely why he plays . . . right into her hands.

So let's practice. Let's pretend you are on a date. Imagine that you are sitting in his car under the moon-light, kissing. While he's putting on the moves he asks, "Where do you see yourself in five years? Do you see yourself getting married?" (Not that he cares. He just has to pretend he's interested in a "meaningful relation-ship" in order to hit the target.) So you answer, "Oh, yes.

I see myself married, with two kids. One boy and one girl." (Cut!!! Wrong answer. Let's rewrite that script and reshoot this scene.)

You have to hit the Snooze button on your biological clock. If a man asks you a direct question about marriage or kids, you have to deflect the question with one of the following:

"Marriage? Who, me?
I suppose if I found someone special
enough I'd consider it.
But he'd really have to be pretty amazing."

"It hasn't crossed my mind.
I guess it would depend on the person
and how we felt about each other."

In other words, act about as enthusiastic as you'd be if he asked you what size engine you have in your car.

The point is to give him *no guarantees*. Also, be sure to interject his favorite word: *fun*. Used in a sentence: "We are enjoying each other and just having *fun*." Here's how the word *fun* translates in the male brain:

No pressure. No expectations. No demands.

At the end of a date, avoid asking, "When will I see you again? When will you call me?" Instead, play up your femininity. Smile, give him a kiss, thank him, and tell him how much you enjoyed yourself. Then be sure to kick him out. Don't forget the magic word: *fun*. He is a "really fun guy." This lets him know you live for the moment. As for what you see in your future? Oops. You can't see past next weekend.

To a woman, this seems like torture or a cruel circus trick. But for a man, this is relationship Utopia and a wet dream come true. Suddenly, he can relax and enjoy himself. "Wow. That's pretty cool. Finally, I can get closer to a woman without having to worry about her locking me down." Now you become that cool dream-woman he's always heard about, but has never met. *Then he lowers his guard and falls in love.*

Therefore, on a date, talk about everything that interests you. Just don't be all up in his grille about relationships, "the future," kids, or marriage.

The opposite is also true. If you never want to go out with a guy again, keep talking about your biological clock. Tell him the fertility doctor said your eggs are popping all over the place. Say "ooh" and "ah" over every newborn you see strapped to a woman's chest. Tell him you want lots of kids, your religion prohibits the use of birth control, and your mom is moving in to help take care of the little ones. (Less expensive than a restraining order, and far more effective.) To seal the deal, buy a card and leave it on his doorstep with a baby rattle and a Winnie the Pooh stuffed animal. Then write, "I can't sleep or eat. I think about you constantly. I can't wait to begin our future together." (See Charlie? See Charlie run . . . .)

The Bitch Convinces Him He "Won" the Commitment

It's one thing not to offer guarantees, but it's something altogether different when two to three months have passed and you still seem *slightly unsure* how he fits into your future. You should continue to be very sweet. That will confuse him because he'll be asking himself, "Wait, why isn't she pressuring me for a commitment?" At some point he'll bring it up. A good thing to say is:

"I really like you but I'm not 100 percent sure. We are still learning about each other."

His immediate response will be, "You aren't sure? What do you mean you aren't sure? I am the brightest, the 'bestest,' and the smartest!" He'll automatically step up his game to win you over. Why? To prove he is a worthy pick. And then you get a twofer. Not only do you get commitment . . . you even convince him that it's *his idea*.

RELATIONSHIP PRINCIPLE 18

If he has no guarantees, becomes attached, and thinks you could be gone at any time, that's when he'll cherish the idea of securing a relationship.

He might become suspicious that other men are pursuing you. And it's good for him to wonder a little. But you should never talk about other men directly. Just be unavailable once in a while, and it will automatically turn the cogs in his imagination.

The reason keeping a little bit of distance makes a man fixate on you is that nine out of ten women *assume the role of girlfriend after a month or two*. First, she starts calling him for his nightly bed checks. Then his socks are rolled up into little balls, and his closet is reorganized. His weekends are filled with weddings, open houses, and baby showers. And before long, he starts to miss football Sundays on the couch with his hands down his pants (to make sure he's still got 'em).

This is why men back off. The adjustment is too drastic, too quick, and too easy. Like he's joined the army, his hair has been shaved off and he has no idea who he is anymore. Now he's no longer "the man." Now he is Bambi in the crosshairs, and the crosshairs are aimed right at his little Bambi balls. So he scurries out the door . . . like he's being shot at.

Remember, you want to discuss commitment, but he does not. Commitment is something a man has to fall into. It's sort of like falling into an eight-foot-deep hole in the ground that he didn't see coming until it was too late. He went out for a nice little stroll and oops . . . lo and behold . . . he fell. "Help! I've fallen and I can't get up!" Now he's stuck to the floor like a peanut butter cup.

RELATIONSHIP PRINCIPLE 19

There's nothing more prized to a man than something he had to wait for, work for, or struggle a little bit to get.

Men are natural-born competitors. And the irony is, when he *doesn't* have you, that's when he thinks the whole relationship is being dominated by him and he's in control of "where it's going." To him, dominance is about getting the woman he really wants. Entrapment is about getting hog-tied by a woman who chose *him*. The latter is emasculating. This is why you want to remain "dumb like a fox" and allow him to think he's in control. Here's how.

How to Convince Him He Is a Winner . . . Almost

- Begin by seeming as if you don't want to hang on to him too tightly. In his mind, this means he isn't "wonderful" . . . yet.
- Then give a little encouragement, but not too much. The best way to do this is with strategically placed compliments. "You are so smart." Now he thinks you admire him, but he's dominating the relationship and is in control of "where it's going."

- Be sure to say, "I really value your opinion. Could I ask your advice?" He will then take a full hour to show you how "manly" he is. No yawning allowed, simply order another drink.
- Be affectionate in public. Touch his lower back when you are waiting in line at the movies. Stand close to him here and there. Touch his hand at dinner. Rub his knee while he's driving, because then his hands are busy on the wheel or the gearshift. Don't do it excessively—just a little. And try to keep sex at bay.
- When he becomes a little more aggressive, don't respond in a "hot and heavy" way. If he gropes your butt or tries to put his hand close to the twins, give him a little bit of play but not too much. Then you can say, "Let me come to you." It's every guy's fantasy: having a woman jump his bones. He'll be patient as long as he feels he's not wasting his time, *and can see a light at the end of the tunnel.*
- If he kisses you and you respond with "ooh baby, oh yes," then he reads it as "She is ready for mounting." But if, instead, you remain cool when he's putting on the moves, then he has to question what it is that you want. *That's where you want to keep him because now he's thinking of how to please you and win you over.*
- *The longer you keep him in a suspended state of not knowing if he's won you over, the more he'll cherish you and the more attached he'll become.*
- Cover pot. Let simmer and bring to a slow boil.

When a man is in pursuit mode, he gets the same feeling he gets when he's playing a slot machine in a casino. He can lose ten times in a row, but he'll still be on the edge of his seat thinking, "I'm almost winning." Every time he thinks he's losing, all you have to do is sweeten the pot. If you ask him to fix something, you make him feel like a winner. If you convince him he had a great idea, he's a winner. If he suggests a shoot-'em-up-bang-bang movie or auto racing, and you say "No, I'm not going," and then twenty minutes later you say "You are right, let's go to an auto race," now he's winning again. He thinks he's dominating the whole show—as long as you make everything *his* "brilliant" idea. He even buys a big fat engagement ring for this reason. Why? So other men will look at the ring and say "I can't compete with that." Now he's a winner again.

Liz and Matt were at a romantic Italian bistro, six months into their relationship. Before dinner was served he said, "Look, I'm not ready for anything too serious. How about you? Do you want to get married?" She came back with a great answer. "Gee, I can't tonight. My dress is at the cleaners and I have to be up early in the morning. But I'm so flattered. Thank you for asking." (A year later, he got up and told that story to the guests at their wedding.)

When a man is left guessing what you want, it makes commitment desirable because he has a chance to bring it up. He also doesn't have to worry, "Is she in love with me, or is she in love with the fantasy?" This is a huge consideration in the commitment equation for a guy.

On the other hand, if you seem to encroach, he'll go into a "holding pattern." A holding pattern means that something has the *appearance* of movement but it really isn't making any headway. Visualize an airplane that is taxiing on a runway, going around in circles, but never takes off. This is what men often do in relationships. They create the appearance that there is progress in the relationship, while putting it on ice. And you sidestep this by ignoring what he says, *by not making it obvious you want a "meaningful relationship,"* and by carefully observing his actions.

Because this is so important, let's do a recap of the typical dating dynamic, *so you recognize the trap you shouldn't be stepping into.*

WHY MEN GET SPOOKED OUT OF WANTING A COMMITMENT

First, he meets a woman he likes a lot. Her independent and slightly elusive aura gives him an important first impression:

"She doesn't need me. She likes me for who I am. Let me get to know her better."

So far so good. If she starts probing about "his intentions" or "the future," he will say:

"Let's get to know each other slowly and see where it leads." Or, "Let's take it one day at a time."

Women will sometimes misinterpret this as rejection. Then she begins to press for more verbal reassurance:

"Where is this going?"
"What do you see in our future?"
"Where do we stand?"

(Now let's hit the Pause button.) Here's why you won't get the response you're looking for. If he's operating on his own time clock, commitment or exclusivity will be something he'll bring up after three to six months. Most women don't wait that long. They bring it up after two to four weeks. A man must feel desired *for who he is* before committing, and in his mind you can't possibly know him well enough after a couple of weeks to make that decision. It has nothing to do with seeing other women or "commitment phobia." He wants to feel it's his unique set of qualities you fell for, and that his "magnificence" and "brilliance" won you over. And that you wouldn't be with just any guy who would take you in. This is the number-one reason why men back off. This is why you need to seem as if you haven't made up your mind. He wants your search to be complete and thorough, because you are discerning and will not settle for second best. If you are in a hurry, he'll think:

"She's insecure and needs to fill a void.
She cannot be alone."

"I'm just filling a position.
She needs me to write checks for her dreams."

"Her attention or desire to secure a relationship has nothing to do with me personally."

That's when the holding pattern and stall tactics begin:

"Space. I need space."

"I'm very busy with work."

"My circumstances need to change before I can commit."

"It's nothing you did, it's all me.
I fell off my bike in the third grade, and my unresolved childhood issues prevent me from committing.
My therapist tells me that too much intimacy would be harmful to my emotional healing."

"I'm just not ready . . . *right now*. But I may feel differently in six to nine months. In the meantime, I could use a little convincing, preferably while naked [pants unzip]. Right here . . . ooh . . . yeah, that feels good. Don't stop . . ."

Anytime you "lobby for a position" or try to move things along, the guy will be reticent to shift gears. This is true after three months or three years. At every interval, you have to make it his idea. Men are hunters. And he has to chase you . . . until you catch him.

Shawn and Theresa are an example of what often happens six or nine months down the road. They were seriously involved for almost a year. He had been married previously. The ex-wife was remarrying and vacating his Bel Air home. Shawn told Theresa he was thrilled to be moving back into his beautiful house. That Sunday, he drove her by the house to show it to her. As they passed it, she instantly blurted, "When you move back in, I'm moving in with you!" Until then, Shawn had been thinking along the same lines. But when she said that, it made him want him to move farther away from her, in the opposite direction. In his mind, it was his decision to make. Not hers.

RELATIONSHIP PRINCIPLE 20

As soon as a woman hands a man a more serious commitment on a silver platter, he'll be reluctant to take it.

This is why you often hear of how men freak out over a woman leaving her toothbrush or a hair dryer at his place. Like in the movie *How to Lose a Guy in Ten Days* or in the saga of Carrie and Big in *Sex and the City*. There are several things women do to "move things along" that men regard as dead giveaways. Women see them as innocent, but men see them as glaringly obvious. When I interviewed men, they said they pick up on even the most subtle nuances. The following list is based on the feedback they gave:

- **Don't introduce him as your "boyfriend" right away.** This suggests to a man that you are setting up for the long haul, and you want to preserve the impression you are still undecided.
- **No lover's gazes.** To you it's romantic. But to him, he's being eyed up like prey no different than the way a lion looks at a gazelle. If you've ever seen a lion look at a gazelle, it hides in the bushes and stares down the gazelle. That's how men feel when you do the goo-goo eyes too soon.
- **With voice messages, shorter is better.** And don't profess your love from the mountaintop. Something familiar or too cozy like, (Beep!) "Hi, pooky wooky I just called because I miss you." Or, "Hi . . . it's just me," or, "You know who this is," after one or two dates can set off bells and whistles. Why? Because of the automatic *presumption* that you two are already an item. When you leave a message, say your name and your number as though it's the first (and last) time you could be calling. This translates: *unobtainable*.
- **Don't give him framed pictures of you for his home and office.** And no shots fired through the ex-girlfriend's photos, either. For

proper disposal of all ex-girlfriend memorabilia, simply wait until you move in together. Between pickup and the scheduled delivery, boxes marked HANDLE WITH CARE shall mysteriously disappear to the dump.

- **Don't mention his family or bring him over to meet yours until *he gets serious with you.*** It never fails. Your great-grandma will call him by every ex-boyfriend's name, remind you that you are "no spring chicken," and ask him when the wedding is. Then she'll scream, "Where's my applesauce!"
- **Don't drop the "L-bomb" within the first couple of months.** You don't love him, you don't love the sex. You *like* the sport coat. Good enough.
- **Don't use new age words like *we, us, ours, destiny, soul mate*, or anything with a "togetherness" feeling.** Don't use catch phrases like *it was meant to be* or the *universe brought you to me*. If he hasn't made up his mind yet, sappy words will scare the daylights out of him. Let him be the first to use those words with you.
- **Don't tell him about your therapy sessions, antidepressant drugs, or childhood issues.** And leave out the one about the bladder-control support group.
- **Don't try to be Mary Poppins or give him the "I'm trustworthy" speech.** Don't tell him you

love charity work, orphans, and old people. Don't say, "I would never lie in a relationship." If you do, he'll know you've just told your first lie.

- **Don't try to rearrange his furniture to make your visits more tolerable.** He'll think you are moving in. Don't try to feng shui his place. Leave it the way you found it: "ghetto shui." The only way he'll get excited about feng shui is if he thinks it comes with free egg rolls and a fortune cookie. Instead, *think like a bitch*. Leave it nice and miserable at his place, so that when he visits your place it will feel like he's "Movin' on Up" like George and Weezy Jefferson.
- **Don't buy wifelike items such as towels or sheets.** If you buy a gift, get something less intimate, like a dog bed for his pet. Besides, when you do move in together, you'll want to liquidate all his crap at a garage sale anyway. Plan it on Super Bowl Sunday when his favorite team is playing. "See those huge boxes over there? All that crap is one dollar. But only if you get everything out of here before half-time . . . ."
- **If he introduces you as his girlfriend, don't gleefully do a victory dance, like you just won the mother lode.** Give him a saucy look and say, "Is that so?"

RELATIONSHIP PRINCIPLE 21

Don't be so blunt, obvious, or available that you come across as having already made up your mind about the guy.

Men *want* love and exclusivity just as much as women do. But he won't go there if it's expected or thrust upon him, *or if he didn't feel he had a choice in the matter*. The less you try to sell yourself, the more self-assured you'll seem. *The whole art of seduction involves the appearance of slight elusiveness*. Just kick back, go out, and enjoy yourself, and he'll come up with all of the above ideas. Your aura should say, "I believe in me." That breaks down in the male hard-wiring: *"She is secure within herself and knows how to handle a relationship."*

The Bitch Mixes It Up

Once you start getting cozy, avoid behaving in a way that allows him to predict your whereabouts at all times. He shouldn't feel that he can always reach you at the same time of day, each and every day. At night, he doesn't get a "round-the-clock booty calling card." If you had to wake up to answer his call, you are not to be joined twenty minutes later. Even during daylight hours, don't allow there to be an "electronic leash" around your neck with 24/7 access.

If you do very early on, it will turn the relationship into a monotonous routine. He'll think, "Okay, I've got this one right where I want her. So let me put her on the backup reserve list and see who else is out there."

RELATIONSHIP PRINCIPLE 22

You want to figure out his pattern, but don't let him figure out yours.

On the flip side, you don't want to make it seem like he is expected to check in, either. The mistake women often make is to try to keep tabs on the guy, which turns calling into a dreaded obligation. If he feels like a GPS tracking system has been attached as an ankle device to assess his longitude and latitude at all times . . . congrats. His guard will go back up (and access to his heart will be denied).

He can't know you expect him to call or that your happiness depends on it. For example, Lauren was at home when Hugh called her, and they made small talk. Then he asked, "What are you doing for the rest of the evening?" Most women make the mistake of saying, "Oh, nothing. Just talking to you, sweetie." Then he thinks to himself, "Gee, doesn't take much to keep her happy" Instead, Lauren told him, "I'm taking a bubble bath, listening to a new CD, and then I'm watching a movie. I can't wait."

RELATIONSHIP PRINCIPLE 23

Men are far more smitten when they feel like they are "stealing" your time away from something else you could have been doing.

It's not so much *how often* you call or whether you occasionally call him, but rather, *how your demeanor seems* when you talk to him. When he calls you . . .

1. ALWAYS ASK POSITIVE, HAPPY QUESTIONS LIKE:

"Hi, how was your day?" "How are you?"

This says: "Tell me something good, sugar pants."

2. AVOID ASKING THINGS THAT SOUND LIKE A BOUNTY HUNTER CLOSING IN ON A FUGITIVE:

"Where did you go when you left work?"

"You didn't tell me where you were. I was worried."

"Why didn't you call?"

"Your cell rang and went to voice mail. Why aren't you answering? Why is it on vibrate?"

This says: "Tell me something bad, you dirty, rotten scoundrel and lying SOB."

Do you feel the difference? The second you shift into expecting a call or getting pissed when he doesn't call you, that's when he'll start to dodge you. But if you are happy and upbeat, he'll keep dropping his guard until he gets deeply attached. The fact that you don't want to intrude will *draw him in a very, very big way*. At the onset, that's your *best* asset—more than sex, and more than beauty.

RELATIONSHIP PRINCIPLE 24

When a woman makes a man feel he's trusted, it makes him feel strong and worthy. It makes him want to be honorable and do the right thing.

Just like you want to feel secure, he wants to feel trusted. It makes him feel comforted and soothed: "This is not a waste of my time. I'm doing something right." It builds him up, and makes him feel like he doesn't want to break that trust. And, it makes him want to protect you even more.

The question women often ask is, "But what if I want him to call me more?" or, "What if I am pissed off he didn't call me at a certain time?" Mia's situation provides a good example of how to effect a change in his behavior. She was used to hearing from John every night. He would get into his car after work at 5:00 and call her while he was stuck in traffic. She started to feel like he was "checking in," like she was just another errand. It became a little *too* convenient. But rather than ask him to make a change, she made a change. She simply stopped answering at 5:00.

If a man can normally reach you at 5:00 and then suddenly cannot, he'll call at 6:00 . . . at 7:00 . . . and at 8:00, or until he gets ahold of you. This is how you turn a boring phone call into an exciting event. Men love it when they are curious and they wonder and get all jazzed about a woman. (And you mustn't deny him such a jazzy good time.)

If you agree to be somewhere or to call him at a certain time, it's very important to keep your word. It's the *random* phone calls you want to alternate. Here are a few more ways to get what you want, without having to nag or explain a word.

IF HE . . .	**YOU SHOULD . . .**
If he takes a few hours to return a phone call . . .	Take a few hours to pick up. Monkey see, monkey do. This will keep the relationship reciprocal and balanced.
If he keeps calling to push back the plans from 5:00 . . . to 6:00 . . . to 7:00 . . .	Agree to the first delay. If he pushes back again, pull the plug politely. Tell him to take care of his business and suggest hooking up later that week.
If he calls hours later than he said he was going to . . .	Let the answering machine pick up. It's amazing how quickly a couple of missed phone calls will make him ask, "Are you mad at me? I thought you were mad at me." (Correct answer: "Not at all. I've been crazy busy.")

If he calls at 9:00 and wants to get together at 10:00 . . .	Tell him you are going to bed early. That will make him plan his outings earlier, with more advance notice.
If he calls after 10:00 or at a time when you would normally be asleep . . .	Wait until your next date and politely tell him not to call you past 10:00. That shows you can live without talking to him, and you aren't that concerned with where he is at night.
If he wants to see you for one or two hours, or just enough time to have sex . . .	Tell him you don't work in "little time frames." Suggest another night when you both have more time.
If he doesn't call you when he's out of town . . .	He shouldn't be able to get ahold of you when he gets back.
If he is in a crabby mood and you aren't enjoying yourself . . .	Give him a kiss on the cheek, tell him you have an early morning, and go home.

Regardless of how many times a week he calls or wants to see you . . . don't be available 100 percent of the time.

RELATIONSHIP PRINCIPLE 25

Men like rules and they like guidelines. If there's something you don't like, he'll respect you for voicing it. He wants to know what the "do's and don'ts" are.

It's actually a huge turn-on to most men when they are with a woman who behaves in a way that shows that she has a full life, and that if he wants to be in her world, he will have to integrate himself into *her* life.

This keeps a marriage spicy too. A girlfriend of mine, Nicole, recently got married to a European guy. Every year, he visits his parents in Europe. When I met her for lunch, she was on the cell phone telling her husband in Germany she was going to see a movie that evening. Then she ended the call and giggled. "He calls me three times a day to see what I'm up to. He wants to make sure I 'behave myself.'" Does she call him overseas? Nope.

Have you ever noticed that men love distracting you when you're on the phone? That's when they love kissing your neck or screwing up your concentration. There's nothing more interesting to a guy than a woman who is distracted or not focused on him.

Being unobtainable or independent is not just about distance or physical proximity. It has to do with how much of your mind space he has access to. You can be living separately and be totally *readable*, or you can be right in the next room and be very mysterious.

For example, Jenny lives with her boyfriend. She was complaining to him that she feels ignored when he watches TV on the couch. Then she did the opposite. She went into the bedroom and started reading a good book. After the third night, he turned the TV off early and climbed into bed, hoping to cuddle. She didn't immediately put the book down. Predictably, he started poking her, playfully hitting her, and acting like a little kid just to get attention *from her.*

RELATIONSHIP PRINCIPLE 26

Men love knowing there's a small part of you that they can't get to.

A married girlfriend of mine, Linda, said that whenever her husband starts ignoring her, she'll go into the bathroom, take out her makeup case, and start putting on her glamour-girl face. Then she'll pick out a nice outfit and spray on some good perfume. Instantly, her husband will become alarmed. "Where are you going all dressed up?" So Linda will say something like, "I'm going to Starbucks to meet Sue. We might go to that new martini club," or, "I'm running some errands." And then he'll ask her again, "You are going dressed . . . *like that*?"

Add to the equation that Linda's husband *knows* when he's being neglectful. So immediately, he worries she might want outside attention. And it never fails. Sometimes he'll seduce her to keep her from going out, other times he'll have dinner reservations or flowers when she gets back.

RELATIONSHIP PRINCIPLE 27

Men read a lot into where you've been, by how dolled up you are when you get home. If you are dolled up and you weren't with him, it will keep him wondering a little.

Sometimes women misinterpret the cliché "Men always want what they cannot have" and assume they have to have a rotation of guys coming around. So let's clarify. He doesn't have to compete with other men. He does have to "win" time from your other interests and all the little things that you like doing.

My girlfriend Helene is a real estate agent who recently got engaged. Her fiancé called and said, "Hey, meet me for happy hour." She told him she couldn't because she had to show a couple of properties at six o'clock. Then he tried to persuade her to cancel her appointments. "Oh, come on. It's happy hour!" And she jokingly quipped, "For me, happy hour is the hour after the check arrives in the mail. When I open up my envelope, I get happy for a whole hour."

The second you put your life on hold, you become less interesting.

The thing to do is set the pattern from the beginning, when he's asking you out on dates. How? When you talk about when to get together, occasionally mention your *block out* times. In other words, the times he *can't* have access to you. This has to be done very subtly. Don't overdo it. But every now and then, throw in one of these.

BLOCK OUT TIMES

"I can't see you on X . . . but I can see you on Y."

For example,

"I can't see you on Wednesday because I promised my girlfriend I'd go to her art exhibit. Want to do it Thursday?"

"This weekend I can't because I've got family visiting. Why don't we do it Tuesday night instead, after they leave?"

"This week is rough. I've got two deadlines at work. Can we get together this weekend?"

"Gosh, Tuesday's not good. Tuesday is my favorite spinning class. Want to do Wednesday night?"

If he sees he is not your only social outlet, he'll keep himself penciled into your schedule. And this has everything to do with marriage, because it demonstrates the most desirable characteristic he can have in a wife: *You are whole within yourself, and you don't need him to validate your self-worth.*

RELATIONSHIP PRINCIPLE 28

The magic formula is to give a little . . .

and then pull back.

Give a little . . . and then pull back.

It's a little like a schoolyard game of tag, and you are "it." If you stand there, he'll stop chasing you. But if you keep moving, he'll keep chasing after you. Even when you are married, it charges up his batteries whenever he can't have full access to you.

When Dolly Parton was asked the secret of being happily married for many decades, she said she just packs a bag and travels whenever her husband seems to be getting a little bit complacent. "That's my secret, honey . . . I just stay gone!"

3

THE SUN RISES AND SETS IN HIS *Boxer Shorts*

How to Start a Fire in Him That He Can't Put Out

It's not premarital sex if you have no intention of getting married.

~GEORGE BURNS

Slow and Steady Wins the Race

Men often have a "Mary Ann v. Ginger" debate about who was more desirable on *Gilligan's Island*. Ginger wore her sex appeal on her sleeve and flirted with everyone on the island. Most men would hump Ginger in the bushes, and not bother helping her out of the bushes when they were finished. On the flip side, most guys would pass on Ginger in a heartbeat if it meant having the *chance* to be with Mary Ann. Why? To most men, Mary Ann was more desirable sexually. She was wholesome. This made their imaginations run wild.

What does this have to do with marriage? For the Ginger type, he'll get a nice hotel room for the night. But for Mary Ann, he'll buy a million-dollar ranch on twelve acres of land, and put two BMWs in the garage. That's the girl he marries. Why? Men are territorial about their wives. With Mary Ann, he doesn't have to worry about her screwing the milkman while he's at work.

RELATIONSHIP PRINCIPLE 29

Women are constantly being told amazing sex will win a man's heart. This is false. Just because a man sleeps with you doesn't mean he cares about you. Nor will good sex *make him care* about you.

It's ridiculous how often you see articles titled "100 Sex Tips That Will Drive Him Wild." Most are so dumb, you feel dumber for having read them. Think about it. It's not really that hard to please a guy. (If he's not horny, make him a sandwich.)

Here's what these so-called experts *aren't telling you:* With adventurous sex that makes you seem like a seasoned pro, he will "hit it and quit it." Why? Because the sex feels *ordinary*.

Let's say, hypothetically, that you followed all 100 suggestions. You busted out with the edible lingerie, the swing, the latex-related items, the bedroom acrobatics, and the furry handcuffs, and you had the disco ball twirling over the bed. Let's say you tied his hands and feet up with your stockings and got on all fours and barked like a dog. Perhaps you wore a sexy costume (*wrongfully* taken from a second-grader who now has nothing to wear for Halloween). The million-dollar question is: Why doesn't it lead to long-term?

HIS FIRST IMPRESSION	WHAT HE SEES IN THE FUTURE
His first thought is, "This is the best it's ever going to be."	No challenge. Nothing else to work hard for.
His second thought is, " It was automatic, and seemed almost routine."	"I wonder how many other guys she's done this with?"
He decides, "What I do will never be better than what she's already experienced."	I am ordinary, therefore the sex is ordinary.

Every guy wants to delude himself into believing that he (in all his splendor) is going to be the one to introduce you to the wonderful world of sex. He'll be the one to teach you something new. And you have never had an orgasm before meeting him, either. So when you suggest positions he's never heard of, he knows you've already been "taught." Then he's thinking, "Why would I want to do tricks taught to her by some other guy?"

When he thinks you may be more seasoned sexually than he is, it automatically makes him think "short term" rather than long term. And most men find it a little emasculating.

That's when they start worrying whether they'll be the one wearing the polka-dot skirt in the family (with polka-dot wedgies to match).

Obviously, his objective at first is to jump into bed. Your objective is to preserve the possibility of long term, and take the long view. And that means there is no need to ride all the rides at Disneyland on your very first visit to the park.

While your foot is on the brake, he'll be breaking out all the stops. Since no guy hands the playbook over to a woman he's trying to seduce, I decided to fly below radar and find out the scandalous tricks men use to heat things up. His first objective? To get past your front door.

HIS PLAYBOOK	YOUR PLAYBOOK
At the end of the night, he may ask, "Can I use your bathroom?"	Let him. Then wait with your winter coat and boots on and the umbrella still open. Don't take off one layer of clothing. Not even your gloves or hat.
He may do a few too many tequila shots and then say, "I'm too drunk to drive, can I sleep on your couch?"	He's hoping you'll say, "I'm not going to let you sleep on the couch, silly. You can sleep in my bed, but only if you behave." Instead, break out the strong Colombian coffee and call him a cab. He doesn't get past the kitchen.
He might offer a massage: "You've been under a lot of stress lately. How about I give you a back rub? I'll be a perfect gentleman, I promise."	After you get warmed up, he'll ask, "Could you unsnap your bra? I just want you to be more comfortable. Can you pull your shorts down to your ankles? I want to be able to massage your lower back. That's where your stress is . . . you poor thing."
He might ask, "Can I come in for a second to use your phone? I need to check my voice mail and my cell phone went dead."	Let him use the phone. After that, be sure he "eases on down the road."

HIS PLAYBOOK	YOUR PLAYBOOK
He may take the platonic approach: "Go change. Get comfortable. Pretend I'm not even here and do what you would ordinarily do if you were by yourself."	His first observation after you change will be, "Damn. She's not wearing a bra or underwear." Then he'll say, "Come lie down on the couch. Get a blanket. Let's just watch TV."
Last, but not least, is the cuddle trick. "I'll stay the night and we'll just cuddle as friends. I promise to leave my underwear on. Scout's honor." Then the story changes: "This underwear is way too constricting. It's itching me. I have to take them off. I hate when this happens . . . do you mind?"	(Game over.) Fast forward ten minutes. "I need to put it in just for a second. I want to know what it feels like to be inside you. We don't have to make love. Just the tip . . . I promise!" And the next thing you know, he's riding you like a Shetland pony.

The nice girl often gives in too early and then tries to do damage control. "I've never done this before. No, really. I don't usually do this with someone I barely know." When men hear this, they assume the opposite. They call it "the antislut defense."

Whenever you hear the words *don't worry* or *trust me*, be afraid . . . be very afraid. That's what the wolf said to Little Red Riding Hood. You should believe everything he says if you still believe in Santa Claus. Whenever a man says, "Don't worry, I promise that I will be a perfect gentleman," what he's saying is "I can't be trusted." If he's truly a gentleman, he doesn't need to announce it.

RELATIONSHIP PRINCIPLE 30

The way to weed out the contenders from the pretenders is to assess their attitude about waiting for sex. If he likes you, he'll be happy just being in your company.

Sex is like his favorite spectator sport: football. He will try to "move the ball" down the field a few yards at a time. Then he gets a new line of scrimmage, a first down, and another opportunity to score. If he struggles, his love of the game is elevated. "Woo-hoo!" Butts get spanked and champagne bottles get popped. *He secretly wants you to give him some resistance.* Because if you just give him the ball and an empty field . . . all the stimulation will be taken out of it.

Paige didn't realize this when she tried to seduce Ted. They had gone out twice but hadn't been intimate. On their third date, they were leaving for dinner when she said, "I went shopping and I want to show you what I bought." Then she pulled out whipped cream and a G-string made out of red licorice. "I hope you like strawberry because we are going to try this stuff out later tonight." Paige thought that Ted would fall out of his tree. "I'll turn him out. He'll never be able to resist me. Then he'll marry me." Instead, it did the opposite: *It accelerated the rate at which he grew tired of her.*

The first way to discern if he's truly interested in you is to take note of how you are spending your time outside the bedroom. Does he spend time with you during the daylight hours? Is he interested in what you like? This is very telling. Even if you like doing something a little boring, like taking your dog to the park, a guy who is really into you will be excited to come along anyway. Silly things will be interesting to him because they are something that you are into, and he finds *you* exciting.

To a guy who wants a partner, a woman who is cautious seems to have more self-worth. Laurie is a perfect example of this. She lives in NYC and Sean commuted to Long Island. After two dinners together, he called her and asked, "Could I sleep on your couch tonight? I have an early morning tomorrow in the city. That way we could go to dinner and I could be a block away from my appointment." Laurie told him she wasn't feeling up to it, and she didn't have to explain why. He got it. And it instantly raised her desirability in his eyes.

The following suggestions will set a classy tone, so he views you as someone he can take seriously.

- **Don't talk about places you'd like to have sex or what your favorite humping music is.** He doesn't marry the girl who tells him, in the first phone conversation, she likes being "spanked by Daddy" with a broken car antenna in the backseat of the car.
- **Plan activities.** Don't start the dating pattern of hanging out and watching videos. Not unless you want dinner reservations to sound like this: "We'll have two cheeseburgers, a large fries, and some Tater Tots. I'll drive around and pick that up at the second window."
- **Dress a little sexy, but not too revealingly.** When you show a little but not everything, his read is, "Now that's a woman who is in control."
- **Avoid heavy petting on the couch or bed until you are 100 percent ready to go the distance.** It's always safe to kiss while standing *vertically* in a door or lobby. There's a reason that they call it the "horizontal mambo."
- **Invite him in *before* you leave for your dinner date.** Let him pick you up at six thirty if the reservations are for seven thirty. Have a glass of wine and let him meet the cat or the dog. This helps break the ice, and prevents late-night access. Then when you send him on his way at the end of the date, it won't seem so impersonal.

- **No crying in your beer about how the ex did you wrong.** Don't say he was a jerk, that he drove too fast, or that he spent all your money. All that does is reduce your worth in his eyes. Leave the "poor me" story out of the conversation. Besides, it's none of his business. If he asks about the ex, simply say, "Long and boring story. [*Yawn.*]" Translation: "Over it."
- **When the kissing starts getting heated and you want to stop, don't say "quit it" or "stop it" or "knock it off" like a whiny young girl.** The *key is to stop him with your body language.* If his hand is trying to do meet-and-greet with your derriere, this is a good time to reach back there and hold that friendly little hand, and then gently ease away. "We'll miss the show if we don't get going." This also exudes that you are a woman in control. Now he is forced to feel respect for you.

It's best to avoid heavy petting on the couch for another reason: If you bring him to the point of no return and then hit the kill switch at the last minute, he'll resent it. Besides, you won't sound too convincing if you say, "Not yet, I want it to be special." Especially if you've been dry humping him for an hour and your hand is keeping it warm in his boxers when you break the news. It's a little too late to stop the fiesta when his tool is doing the cha-cha, and the "Boot Scootin' Boogie" in his britches.

RELATIONSHIP PRINCIPLE 31

The purpose of waiting is not just to seem classier. You also want to give yourself time to observe him and find out key facts about him.

. . . Like whether he has a wife and three kids in another state. Or whether all his friends are hoodlums. You want to figure out whether the ex-girlfriend is still having "breakup sex" with him (because she doesn't know they've broken up yet). And you want to find out about his college days, and whether he's ever gone roller blading through the streets of San Francisco wearing Daisy Dukes and a leotard.

Time allows you to smoke him out. See who he is. And don't adopt the philosophy of Sir Isaac Newton, who said, "What goes up must come down." Don't apply that rule to sex. Remember the sign you see when you walk into a place of business:

"We reserve the right to refuse service to anyone"?

Hang that one on your bedroom door.

We Reserve the Right to Refuse Service If:

IF HE IS TOO AGGRESSIVE

If he's interested in you, he won't be too grabby or proposition you on the first couple of dates because he won't want you to think he's a pig. If sex is all *he's focused on, that demonstrates going in that he's not concerned with who you are. If a little resistance is too much for the guy and he takes off, you are better off. In fact, clear a path for him and make sure there's nothing in his way on the way out.*

IF HE WON'T STAY THE NIGHT

Don't sleep with a guy who tells you, "I can't stay the night," or a guy who tells you that you can't stay at his place. This guy is already warning you before you have sex that he intends to keep you at arm's length. If you are making out and he says, "I can't stay over," that's your cue to say, "Who said you were staying over?"

IF THERE ARE TOO MANY "QUEENS IN THE CASTLE"

Don't get sexually involved with him if he makes it obvious he has a harem of female "friends" waiting to come in off the wings and take your place. And it doesn't matter if he swears they are "just friends." Listen to your gut.

IF YOU DON'T FEEL COMFORTABLE

Your instincts are the most valuable thing you have. Never, ever allow anyone to talk you out of what you feel. As Kim Basinger said: "I feel there are two people inside me—me and my intuition. If I go against her, she'll screw me every time, and if I follow her, we get along quite nicely." Nothing is more important than your body and your health. Treat them like they have some worth.

The nice girl knows that certain guys are "hit and run" artists, but they get seduced by the naughty-girl element. Not before long, she starts convincing herself there is a potential for a relationship. "It will be different with me! I will be the one to reform this guy. I can change him."

For example, he'll be on the bed with a woman making all the moves. Then she'll stop and say, "Wait. I feel like things are moving too fast. I barely know you." So the guy lies back on the bed and says, "Okay, ask me anything you want to know, and I'll tell you. I am an open book." (It's like a sales negotiation. Find out what the objection is and then overcome the objection.) So he tells her a sob story about how his first love broke his heart, and how *used* he felt. Then he shows her the scar on his leg, or how his parents liked his older brother better. Then he touches her cheek gently like he's Fabio. "We don't have to have sex if you aren't ready," he says (while he's thinking, "What other B.S. can I come up with to get her in the sack?"). What does she say? "I am ready! I am yours!" And next thing you know, the downstairs neighbors have plaster falling down off their ceiling until 2:00 A.M.

Fast forward one week for a "state of the union" address. "I don't know why he's not calling. He said we had a connection. It was emotional. He said it wasn't sex . . . it was making love. He said I was special. Maybe we just got off on the wrong foot. Maybe we're just going through a little rough patch in our relationship."

RELATIONSHIP PRINCIPLE 32

Who he *tells* you he is in the beginning has very little to do with how he will *treat* you. If there's sex involved, he'll promise you things you've never even heard of.

Dating Web sites are notoriously misleading for this reason. When a guy is asked to check the box to indicate what type of match he's looking for, which one do you think he's going to check if he just wants sex?

- Casual sex with no protection, and no phone call the next day.
- Commitment, love, and poems under a tree.

He'll check the one that says "commitment." Because he is very committed (to seeing you naked).

After all, men are hunters. We're dealing with a red-blooded hunting creature that prides himself on his ability to conquer. If it were legal, men would have their ex-conquests' heads mounted on the wall, in the den. A bighorn sheep . . . a moose . . . a ten-point deer . . . Jennifer . . . Natalie . . . and a fling named Vanessa (because one-night stands get mounted too).

The actor Vince Vaughn is quoted as saying, "If I'm not interested in a woman, I'm straightforward. Right after sex, I usually say, 'I can't do this anymore. Thanks for coming over!'" No guy is going to say, "I would never marry you. But I really want to get laid." If he's not sincerely interested in you, it's not uncommon for him to say what you want to hear. "Marriage? Kids? A big house? I can hardly wait." Whichever ear it hits first, make sure it flows all the way through and makes its way out the other ear.

So, as the "huntee," the intelligent choice for you is not to roll around on the bed or couch until you really get to know the guy. Wait until you feel comfortable. Give him some time to *show* you—not just *tell* you—who he is with his *actions*.

Dinners, flowers, and being a gentleman—these are the basics if he sees you as the girl of his dreams.

The Heat Between the Sheets

When you become lovers, it's still important to understand that men are evaluating the long-term potential of the relationship. First and foremost, what most men are looking for is a woman who is natural in bed and who genuinely enjoys sex with him. So I asked men, "What are the clues that a woman isn't into it?" Here is some of the feedback they gave:

Clues You Aren't Really Into the Sex

- John said, "A lot of women scream in a pitch that would stop a charging rhino dead in its tracks. They flip their hair around, strike exotic poses, and put on a stage performance. It's like they think they are being videotaped and there's a professional film crew in the room. Lights . . . camera . . . action!"
- Marcus said, "Try not to make it obvious you're watching the clock or keeping track of time. Before sex, don't say, 'It's eight forty-five. We have to stop in fifteen minutes, because *Desperate Housewives* starts at nine o'clock.'"
- Kent said, "Most guys would much rather have an attractive woman who is really into the

sex than a supermodel who isn't really into it. Hands down."

- Frank said, "You know the woman is not all there when she's screaming and hyperventilating, and you haven't even put it in yet. So I'll stop what I'm doing to see what kind of noises she's going to make. If she's screaming and I'm not even touching her, I feel like I can go grab a sandwich and then come back and pick up where I left off."

Men tend to assume that the theatrical performance has nothing to do with their performance. He'll think, "Well, I see she's not into me." And as soon as he gets the vibe you are *not* enjoying the sex, it will be a deal breaker in regard to commitment.

There's no panel of judges giving you a score: "I give a 9.0 for artistic showmanship but a 7.8 for technical performance." If he makes you feel that way, that means he's a lousy lover—not you. With a good lover, you don't worry about whether you need a boob job or whether he can see the cellulite on your left butt cheek, because the guy has you sufficiently distracted.

Interestingly, almost all the men I spoke with said that they rarely pay attention to a woman's flaws until she points them out to him. They find the female form beautiful, and they are admiring what's right. So when he runs his hand across your stomach and you say, "I'm doing crunches and it will be flat by summer," he assumes you are busy scrutinizing your own body, and not thinking about his.

According to men, another mistake women make is that they try to act prim and proper, and virginal. This makes men suspicious. He's no altar boy, and he knows you are no virgin. You'll seem classier if you say nothing about your previous lovers. Besides, even a third-grader can do the math. (Mr. Rogers' music.) "Good morning, boys and girls. Today we have a word problem. If the ratio of men to women is equal, and all the men have had sex with dozens of women, is it mathematically possible that all women have had sex with only three men? The child who cracks this unsolved mystery will win a gold star and a cap with a propeller on top."

The way men infer that you are loose is not by what you say. They judge by how sophisticated your technique is the first time you are intimate. If you want him to see you as his long-term love, you can't make it seem like half the cast of Noah's Ark has been inside your bed. So don't try to come across as the expert humping champion.

Rest assured, he'll pick up on any little sign that you've recently returned from a humping spree. Hence the need for us to take a tour of the bedroom to ensure that you come across as classy. Think of it as a little "tour-de-virgin."

LA TOUR-DE-VIRGIN

- The first time you have sex, don't recycle previously worn hoochie gear. Wear that stuff later on, and make sure he sees you take it out of the bag with the price tags still attached. (I'm serious. Save the bag.) Until then, a pretty lace bra-and-panty set under your clothes is fine. Don't bolt into the bathroom and change into a Madonna corset with a lime-green thong and a studded dog collar. It will seem too rehearsed, and *too* premeditated.

- Never open a drawer where you keep exotic novelties, like a battery operated turbo toy. If it's bigger than a baseball bat and comes with a clutch and a gear shift, it will ruin the warm and fuzzy ambience. After all, you don't want him feeling like a puddle-jumping Cessna airplane parked next to a 747 jumbo-jet.

- Let him suggest the sexual positions the first couple of times. If you break out sexual acrobatics (that have him saying "ouch") and commence to steady riding *him* like a cowboy, he'll think, "This one has been to a few rodeos."

- Don't be in a mad rush to fling your clothes off in every direction and jump right into mounting position. Let him be the one to undress you . . . *slowly*. It will keep you from looking like a horn dog.

- Let him supply the condom. And whatever you do, don't do any tricks where you put the condom in your mouth and then seductively put it on his private parts. "Look at me, Mom! No hands!" He'll think you enrolled and got your "ho" certification. That will guarantee that he'll classify you as short-term. Act like you wouldn't even know where to buy a condom much less identify what one looks like.

- If he didn't bring a condom, never let him see where you hide yours. He can't see the Value Pack from Costco that started out with five hundred condoms (and is now 75 percent empty). Even if it's a twelve-pack and there are six missing, that's six times someone else was inside you. (Not exactly a "mine only" ambience.)

- If he complains about wearing a condom, never say, "*All my boyfriends* wear them and I never have sex without one." If you have a child, don't say, "You have to wear one because I get pregnant really easily." (That will serve to clarify why the Value Pack is now 75 percent empty.)

- Men like women who are girlie. They love lightly scented lotions and anything soft and feminine. (If he sees you have a restraint system on the bed, it might concern him a bit.)

- All men are very insecure about their size. If he's not gifted, you can't look at it and blurt out, "Is that all?" It's in the fine print of your contract. You are required to say, "Ooh. Oh boy. I just can't handle all that. Easy, easy. You are going to knock my back out of alignment."

- Don't ask for constant reassurance. Instead of "Am I doing this right?" ask, "Do you like that?"

- The first time he stays over, don't look like you were too prepared with the overnight kit, or that you are *used to* male sleepovers. Don't put out extra boxers, a razor, and a toothbrush. Also, don't leave the PETCO products in the shower. If the other stuff is strawberry scented, he'll use the flea-and-tick shampoo by mistake.

- Don't serve a five-course breakfast in bed. If you own a magazine that has a picture in it with a breakfast tray, poached eggs, and lilies from the garden—throw it out as a preventative measure so you don't get any bright ideas. Instead, direct him to the nearest coffee shop and ask him to bring you back a caffé latte. And a pretty cookie.

- During pillow talk don't whisper in his ear, "You complete me," or, "I always knew we'd be together." He shouldn't feel he was seduced by *you*. He wants to feel he did the conquering, not the other way around.

Several men also said that they like input from a woman in bed. However, they don't want you to give them a report card or a play-by-play the next day. You can't do the Monday morning postgame review with a pointer in your hand, and a huge chalkboard on the wall, like the guy is retarded. "This is your position X . . . *here*. This is the hopeful O. *That's me*. When I call the play, your objective will be to run, find the hole, and focus on the G-spot."

For all ego-intensive purposes, any Monday-morning quarterbacking will crush him. Show him or tell him what you want *during* the act . . . or forever hold your peace. Tact is important, especially when dealing with his performance and his "best friend." Therefore, I asked men what women need to know when giving a guy pleasure (down under). Here are a few of the penile-code infractions men shared.

The Penile-Code Infractions

- Martin said, "In the middle of giving a B.J. never look up with a cross-eyed look and ask dumb questions. 'Are we close? How much longer is this going to take? What are you thinking?' It's like building a fire and then throwing cold water on it."
- Paul said, "Don't try to buy time, stall, hold it, or have a meaningful conversation with it. It's not one of the Muppets or an Oompa Loompa. Don't use words like *cute* or *adorable* to describe it, or give it a pet name like Little Skippy."
- Christopher said, "When women prop their head up for support, they need to be careful of where they lean their elbow. If your elbow is stabbing a main artery in his thigh, it could cause a slightly distracting numbness in his toes." (Then "twinkle toes" might need to walk it off before you get yours.)

- Allen said, "Look happy. Don't look as if you wanted to complain but couldn't because your mouth was full. At the very least, try to look a little happier than a cat choking on a hairball."

It's official. I think it's safe to say I've blown my chances of ever getting a Pulitzer. Although, there is still a scintilla of a chance I might get a humanitarian award for sharing this next story.

Bobby told me a story about Charlene, who committed a cardinal no-no with the male privates. Charlene was lying on the bed enjoying the afterglow of sex. Bobby had gotten up and was getting dressed. As he bent over to pick up his socks he put one leg up on a chair. Charlene thought his "little trinkets" looked cute and thumped them from behind to see if they would swing. As his knees buckled, he began to hyperventilate and see stars. Psychic hotline prediction: If you do this, you will not hear wedding bells, because he will disappear and stay gone forever. (Nor will he remember you with great fondness and nostalgia.)

With respect to pillow talk, silence is golden. Don't ask questions like "Was it special? Do you love me? Was it good? How good? Better than that other girl? The best you ever had?" If the first thing he hears after a good pump and grind is "That was so much better than that other guy . . . he was a two-pump chump," he'll feel like one of many. He doesn't want to picture you with any other guy, so don't make any comparisons—good or bad. Out of sight . . . out of mind.

Also, don't believe what he says when he professes his love to you right after sex. If he starts talking about "the future," what he really means is it was really good for him too . . . and he wants to try a different position (in the future).

The After-Party

Women are told that as long as they wait out the five-date rule or the requisite one-month time period before having sex, a man will automatically commit and the "deal has been sealed." She's thinking, "All the games are over. I've reached the goal line. We are now a couple." Right? Don't run out and buy matching "his and hers" terry-cloth bathrobes just yet. After sex . . . you're only at halftime, sister.

Let's rewind. You got down and dirty and it was good. And now he thinks he's Joe Stud in the bedroom. The morning after, he's cockier than a peacock in prime mating season. He's singing "We Are the Champions" in the shower. "She left walking with a limp. Her legs are probably still quivering. She'll never be able to *think* about sex again without envisioning my face with a halo around it." In his mind, you've been intimate so he thinks he has all the power. (That's about to change.)

When I interviewed men, I posed the following question: "What would happen if a woman just behaved no differently after sex? What if she was pleasant, but went on about her business like nothing had changed?" (I wish I could videotape their reactions and play them back for you.) Some men turned white. One guy said, "That would turn my world upside down." Most admitted it would freak them out. (Good to know.)

To better understand the "his and hers" after-party dynamics of what's going on immediately after sex, let's review a play-by-play.

The Postsex Play-by-Play

WHAT HE FIRST ANTICIPATES RIGHT AFTER SEX

He's been through the drill with other women and knows that after sex you are likely to expect boyfriend-like behaviors. He will pull back simply because he thinks that a lot will be expected of him. Act like you expect absolutely nothing. *Don't be more, or less, affectionate. Act no differently. Be the same girl. Here's why that will work to your advantage.*

WHY HE'LL PULL BACK

Men want to postpone commitment. He'll alter the dating pattern to avoid regularity and consistency. Why? Because to him, regularity + continuity = commitment. This is why he may pull back, make the rules, break them, switch the rules, and then do another changeup. He'll call more randomly. He'll try to see you on short notice. And he'll try to keep you in second-guessing mode.

HOW HE THINKS YOU'LL RESPOND TO HIS PULLING BACK

He's expecting you to be available 100 percent of the time. When you push, *or you are doting, clingy, or want time and reassurance right after the first time you have sex, he will think that pulling back and keeping you at arm's length is justified. And then he'll make himself scarce.*

WHAT YOU SHOULD DO

Do the opposite. Stay on the go. Don't pick up the phone all the time. If he calls and you are busy, tell him you will call him back. Stay busy with your own life. Don't be available at the last minute or seem ready to go anytime he wants to see you.

WHAT MESSAGE THIS SENDS

You won't be doing all the heavy lifting in the relationship. Now it becomes a relationship of value to him because he sees that you aren't willing to jump into something and give yourself away, just because of one night of passion. Now he sees you as a cool person, not an insecure woman making demands.

WHY THIS LEADS TO COMMITMENT

He'll think, "If she's not freaking out, I guess things weren't progressing as fast as I thought they were." Then he'll revert to his original routine and continue to pursue you.

WHY THIS IS THE ULTIMATE COUP DE GRÂCE

It's a mild ego blow. Now you have his full attention. He's thinking, "That's odd, I thought I was Mack Daddy in the sheets. My phone should be ringing off the hook. What's going on here? Why isn't she chasing me like all the rest of them?"

A woman who behaves more coolly and casually after sex *is the exact opposite of what he is used to experiencing*. If a guy doesn't call you after he's been having crazy sex with you, it's because he is expecting a needy reaction. He's fearing intensity and neediness. Getting the opposite will throw him for a loop and change his orientation very quickly. Now he realizes you are stronger than the rest: "She has standards. She is not a weakling. She is not giggly, stupid, or naïve. She's nobody's pushover."

He'll also wonder why you aren't asking the typical questions he's used to hearing:

- Are we exclusive?
- Are we still cool?
- What's wrong?
- You seem distant.
- Are you mad at me?
- Is everything okay?

You want him to ask these questions of you. When you don't become needy, he'll become fixated on why you *aren't* fixated. "Wait a minute. Why isn't she screaming or asking me where I've been? Maybe she was holding back. Maybe it takes more to impress this one. I better step up my game."

RELATIONSHIP PRINCIPLE 33

When you aren't mind-blown after sex, and you continue to focus on your own life, he'll automatically start looking at you differently. Then he'll start wanting to secure a relationship with you.

It's like child-rearing. During the first year, psychologists say, you should "enthrone" the toddler. After one year, you are supposed to dethrone the toddler to keep him or her from having a really bad case of the "terrible twos." The same can be applied to men. After sex, you have to make sure that he doesn't think he's the only one running the show. If he does, chances are you won't be headed toward a commitment.

A lot of women think that the way to reduce themselves to a booty call is to sleep with a guy too soon. But it really has more to do with *how available she is after sex*. She's thinking that after sex, he's died and gone to heaven. She's expecting Hallmark cards, poems under a tree, and walks on the beach. She gets her hair done for him, dresses for him, and even suffers third-degree burns from her bikini wax to have a pretty "poodle clip" for him. That's when a woman is most likely to be at a man's beck and call. He says, "Baby, I miss you. Can I come over?" (Translation: "I'm horny.") She thinks, "He's my boyfriend now, so what's the harm?" Here's the harm: You are relaxing the standards. And if you do it once or twice? Congrats. You've just set a late-night pattern.

RELATIONSHIP PRINCIPLE 34

After sex, behave as if the relationship is still new.

Men respect anything that they have to invest effort into. It's no different than a teenager with a new sports car. If you hand the keys to an expensive luxury convertible to a sixteen-year-old on a silver platter, he'll get into all kinds of trouble. He'll get speeding tickets, he'll bang it up, and he won't take care of it. But if the same kid has to go out and mow some lawns, trim some trees, and flip a few burgers over the summer, he'll be much more protective of that car. If a buddy of his says, "Hey, let's burn some rubber and see how fast this will go," he'll say, "Are you crazy? I worked all summer to buy these tires."

Michael told a very simple yet poignant story about how his fiancée, Kate, won his respect because she kept her presence of mind after sex. The first weekend they were intimate, Kate got a call from her aunt on Sunday morning from South America. She told Michael that it might take a while. Five minutes passed before he started clearing his throat to hint that he wanted her to get off the phone. Kate covered the receiver and whispered, "Do you have something else you need to take care of? Please don't let me keep you if you need to go."

Certainly not the advice one might anticipate reading in a Miss Manners column, which would probably advise you to say, "How rude of me. I will jump off the phone and fetch your slippers too!" Kate gave Michael the vibe that said he was free to go—in stark contrast to most women, who typically dote on the guy. What it showed was: "I'm not going to stop being who I've always been because of a night of passion. This is my world and I'm not going to stop living the way I always have."

RELATIONSHIP PRINCIPLE 35

Men are intrigued by anything they do not completely control.

And when you are upset or sprung, he knows he's in control. So cool your jets. Chill. After sex, just do what guys do: Make a sandwich. Watch a little ESPN. Order Pay Per View wrestling. Watch *SportsCenter*. And then fall asleep on the couch, in that worn-in spot with the butt imprint on it.

Don't agree to let him stop by without calling. Let him put forth some effort. If you pick him up at the airport at midnight, drop him off at his place and split. Regardless of the reason, don't be a late-night convenience. In the South, they have the slang phrase *go stupid*. After sex, don't go stupid on him. Make him treat you with respect.

Don't assume, "That's how guys are. They don't plan things in advance. They don't go out of their way." Wrong. Does he miss the kickoff at the Super Bowl? Absolutely not. If something is important, it gets priority. On the big game day, he'll be checking the batteries in the remote, making sure the beers are on ice, and warming up that favorite worn-in spot on the couch . . . an hour before the coin toss.

When you don't chase him, he'll come looking for "his girl." Dana and Adam are the perfect story of how a man will come and track you down. They had just slept together and Adam told her he was splitting town with the boys. "I'm going away. [Then he eyed her expecting a response.] Do you have any feelings on this?" He expected her to flip out and reassured her that his cell phone would be on all weekend, but she didn't call.

That Saturday night, she went out with the girls. When she came in, there were nine missed calls and four voice mails. (Notice: It doesn't matter how busy he is. If he wants to reach you, he'll find time to call.) The following morning, Dana returned home from church to find Adam sitting outside on the front steps of her apartment.

RELATIONSHIP PRINCIPLE 36

When you maintain a bit of privacy and he has to wonder a little where you are, you are stimulating his imagination. The second he can't get ahold of you he'll send out an APB, or "all points bulletin," to find you.

Jacqueline Kennedy Onassis said, "There are two types of women: those who want power in the world, and those who want power in bed." And there's a third type: the bitch. She gets both.

*Keeping the Home Fires Burning**
**For Advanced Bitches Only*

Picture a guy walking by the water cooler at work. He overhears two secretaries talking and one says, "I'm not giving him any." Instantly, his ears perk up and it gets stored in his memory bank. There are certain attitudes women have toward sex that register with a man. Here's why the whole idea of "giving him some" doesn't go over well. If he's a good lover, he wants to believe that he's giving you as much pleasure as you are giving him. And that that "somethin'" is hard to resist.

That said, there are times you don't want to have sex. After all, women just aren't as physically strong. We can't lift a heavy box like they can, we can't open a jar—and sometimes we just don't have the physical fortitude to be a pin cushion after a long hard day of chasing kids or meeting work deadlines. If you explain it to him, be sure to do it in a way that makes him feel big and strong while presenting yourself as the delicate little flower. This way you can negotiate a foot massage or a shoulder massage and avoid making him feel rejected. If he feels rejected on an ongoing basis, he will eventually disconnect from the relationship.

RELATIONSHIP PRINCIPLE 37

To a man, a relationship without sex represents a relationship with no love, no affection, and no emotional connection.

Since most women don't have the same sex drive as men, the frequency of sex often becomes an issue. The way to avert this is to keep him surprised sexually. Then he gets physical and mental stimulation, and is a little off balance. When a man can anticipate that he will have sex twice a week at a particular time and in a particular position, he'll begin to feel resentful, as though he's been put on a sexual Slim-Fast diet. But when you keep him surprised, he's always flashing back to the images of hot moments you've recently shared.

RELATIONSHIP PRINCIPLE 38

Always preserve the mystery. Keep the sex sporadic and unpredictable. It makes it much more intense for a man.

Now, instead of the predictable "turkey tidbits on Thursdays," he feels like he is never too far from an all-you-can eat buffet. If you have sex in the hallway on Tuesday and surprise him in the laundry room on Friday—the memories will be burned in his mind. Guys don't forget stuff like that. Now the *mental foreplay* is ongoing 24/7—even though you're still having sex only twice a week.

Never underestimate the power of what you say to a man, before or after sex. A man will put far more value in a relationship and feel more connected to you when you genuinely enjoy the sex and make him feel his "stuff" is extra-special. If you crush his ego, "big daddy" will quickly become "crabby daddy." And then he'll want no part of a commitment.

After all, the way to his heart isn't through his stomach . . . it's through his boxer shorts.

4

Female Button Pushing:

A TIME-HONORED MALE TRADITION

Why Men Deliberately Annoy Women to Figure Out Where They Stand

Well, you know, boys. A nuclear reactor is a lot like women. You just have to read the manual and press the right button.

~HOMER SIMPSON, ON *THE SIMPSONS*

Taking Back the Remote Control to Your Emotions

If you were a fly on the wall listening to a group of men talking, it wouldn't be uncommon to hear them discuss how men are "logical" and women are loose cannons with no emotional control. Like apple pie and baseball, commiserating with his peers ranks among his all-time favorite pastimes. Drinking . . . golfing . . . hunting . . . fishing . . . and some good old-fashioned female-story swapping.

This is why men love the Jack Nicholson line from the movie *As Good As It Gets*. When Nicholson's character is asked how he can write a woman's temperament so well, he responds, "I think of a man. Then I take away all reason and accountability." This is how many men perceive women.

It's the dirty little secret they don't want you knowing about: A guy will annoy you deliberately, egg you on, and then be alert to your response. He'll consciously probe around the edges of your "nice girl" facade to see what he will be dealing with. He wants to know what your backbone is like. He wants to see how alert and smart you are. He wants to see if you recognize when he behaves poorly.

No guy will come in at the end of a bad day and say, "Honey, I need spooning and cuddle time." Instead, he may try to get attention by provoking you. Then he figures out where he stands by how emotional you become. *When you are upset he knows you care and he knows he's in control.*

RELATIONSHIP PRINCIPLE 39

When a woman reacts emotionally, men get three things: attention, control, and the feeling of importance.

In the real world, relationships don't exactly go down like a G-rated plot about sunshine and puppy dogs. Whereas women see no logic in purposefully pissing someone off, men see testing as a tool. I affectionately refer to this process as a "testofest."

Testofest

A strategic, premeditated dating ritual that involves pushing your buttons. The test usually begins with his pulling back in some way just to see what will happen. He may deliberately forget to call.

He may look at another woman. In each instance, he's evaluating your response. He's expecting an *involuntary reflex* caused by a lack of emotional self-control.

After all, relationships don't always come in neat little packages. And sometimes a man will push your pressure points just to see how you react. The second he sees supercharged emotions that he thinks are disproportionate to the perceived snub, you'll quickly get categorized as a woman who can't be taken too seriously. If your feet stomp, tears squirt across the room, and you start screaming in a pitch that would stop a charging rhino, *he will know how much power he has over you*. And:

RELATIONSHIP PRINCIPLE 40

When you are easily manipulated, he will assume he doesn't have to give as much in the way of a commitment in order to keep you there.

If, on the other hand, you don't become unhinged and you respond with a level head, he'll see it as a sign of strength. His trust and respect will deepen, and he'll want to take the relationship to the next level. Instantly, he'll shift gears because he'll realize he's dealing with *an equal.*

For example, let's say a guy comes home after a really rough day at the job. He won't say, "Darling, I need attention." Instead, he'll get into a verbal skirmish with you. And, he gets the feeling of satisfaction after you kiss and make up. This encourages him to use you as an emotional punching bag. On the other hand, you can give him no reward. Say, "Okay. I can see you've had a crummy day. I'll let you wind down and I'll be back in an hour. I'll put a beer in the freezer for you. By the time you get out of the shower it will be really cold. See you later." Then split, and stay gone for two hours. Then you will have his full respect. Why? He's thinking, "That was smooth. She saw it coming and read me like an open book. Hmm . . . she sure sidestepped that. I guess being a jerk will get me replaced."

RELATIONSHIP PRINCIPLE 41

The best way to set limits with a guy when he's testing you is by controlling the ebb and flow of your attention. An emotional reaction is always a reward, even if it's negative attention.

In his mind, he doesn't think he's being a jerk, because he has a specific purpose. So he probes around the edges to find out:

- What are the important things about her that I don't know about yet?
- What will she be like when she's at her worst, or when she feels wronged?"

It's a cross between a "gotcha" game and Pop Goes the Weasel. (Hint: you are the weasel.) He's looking to see if you'll be able to hold your own or whether you will fall apart like a five-year-old having a tantrum at Toys "R" Us.

Remember, there is a fine line between testing and disrespect. So let's do a quick side-by-side comparison.

A TEST	VERSUS DISRESPECT
Usually early on after sex, he will pull back to see how you'll react.	Disrespect is repeated and continual. His inattention is more blatant, more mean-spirited, and usually a sign that the relationship has eroded over a period of time.
He'll call and cancel a date, just to see how you respond and whether you'll be flexible.	He won't call. He'll just stand you up and call a day or two later with a really elaborate half-baked story.
He'll glance at another woman to see how you react, hoping you'll cling to him more tightly.	He'll talk to another woman for the whole evening at a party, with little or no regard for how you feel.
He may tease you playfully, or jokingly harass you or banter with you.	He will be deliberately hurtful, denigrating, or insulting.
He may show up late.	He'll be MIA. After he's missing in action for a week at a time, he'll pop back up on the radar and call you out of the blue and act like nothing is wrong. Usually the call will come late at night.

In a sense, there is no such thing as a "little bit" of disrespect. Because when a man sees that you'll accept a little, it entices him to even greater audacity. The fastest way to become despondent is to let someone push you around, because when you come out of the fog, you'll hate yourself for allowing it. So you have to identify what's happening before you can learn how to respond.

The first question becomes: Should you stand up for yourself verbally? Or nonverbally? To avoid playing into his hands, you have to be a bitch with your actions, not your words.

RELATIONSHIP PRINCIPLE 42

Men *hear* what they *see*.

In the movie *Million Dollar Baby* Morgan Freeman said, "Sometimes the best way to throw a punch is to *take a step back*." The following sections will teach you how to gracefully do just that.

Female Button 1: He may attempt to make you jealous of another woman.

In England, there is a proverb: "A woman without jealousy is like a ball with no bounce." This may help explain why men use jealousy to test women. "How much bounce will she have? Will she be like a pinball machine with bells and whistles? Can I get away with murder if I buy her a dozen roses?" If so, that's great fun. For one person, that is. Men know competitiveness is a weakness of most women, which makes jealousy the Cadillac of all the buttons they can push.

One of the first things a man may do is try to convince you that all his ex-girlfriends still want him (even the one who ran off with another woman). His version? "I let her down easy, but she never got over me." If he spends the day at the zoo, the female gorilla wanted him too. In other words, he wants to hoodwink you into believing every woman between the ages of eighteen and eighty wants him so you'll think he's a catch.

This is why they'll take you to a restaurant and be extra suave to the waitress. Or he'll glance at a woman at the movies. This is why he'll give an extra-long hug to a female friend right in front of you. And not the pat-on-the-back kind of hug, either. It's always the kind of hug that makes you want to spray-hose them down like you're breaking up a couple of dogs.

Carmen was dating Sam for several months. He wanted to see where he stood and decided to broach the subject by telling her about a new girl at work. "There's this girl in my department who is always hitting on me and leaving me notes." (The red flag is that he's announcing it. That's clue number one that it's nothing to be concerned about.) Carmen said, "I sympathize with you. And I know how annoying that can be. I have this body-builder guy who keeps bugging me too. He wants me to go to Europe with him, and I barely even know the guy."

RELATIONSHIP PRINCIPLE 43

When a man tries to make you jealous, it rarely has anything to do with his desire for someone else. When you are upset he gets the reassurance that you care.

Think about it: If he truly had action on the side, would he be telling you? He may as well take out a billboard that says, "I have no action on the side *whatsoever*. And I get plenty of 'me' time in the shower." If a man does something *that* obvious—like leave a woman's business card in *plain view* where he knows you'll see it—he's most likely doing it to get attention and reassurance that you care. The card was put there so you would see it. If a man looks at another woman when you are six inches away from him, you can't be thinking, "Radar! Radar! Another woman is better than me. I am not good enough." He's doing it because he knows you'll pick up on it.

Therefore, apply the Hollywood axiom: "*No audience . . . no show*." If you don't provide a reaction you won't encourage and reinforce the bad behavior.

A classic example is Gary, who took Lindsay to a

company Christmas party and then left her alone to go talk to a few attractive female co-workers. He stayed gone for forty minutes. What some women would have done is stand next to the punch bowl all night, pouting. But Lindsay adopted the "monkey see, monkey do" approach, and acquainted herself with the handsome single men in the room. When she spilled her drink, she was surrounded by men who were trying to pat her dry. Gary turned around, and described it as a "pack of wolves swooping in on my tender little sheep." His sidebar ended as he made a beeline back to his invited guest. Did he leave Lindsay alone at parties after that? Not a chance.

Another variation of the jealousy button is the guy who says, "You know, the one thing I miss about my ex is that she was a really good cook." Allow me to translate: He is hungry. He wants you to go to the kitchen and become the Iron Chef. He's hoping you'll make a big banquet fit for a king, all to compete with some fantasy ex that never even existed. He may say, "She kept a clean house." *Whatever he wants you to do more of, that's what she was allegedly good at.* This is why some men rave about their mother's cooking to their wives—to keep the hot meals coming.

A girlfriend of mine who is a single mother has a twelve-year-old son who visits his father regularly. Then he comes home and raves about his stepmother's cooking: "Candace makes the best fried fish." So you see, it starts early. (That's some unsuspecting little girl's future husband in training.)

This reminds me of a cute story about a girlfriend of mine. She convinced her husband that she was a gourmet cook without ever cooking him a meal. How? One day, she went to a yard sale and picked up a whole box of cooking items for ten dollars. She got a whole pot set, cooking timers, big syringes, and plenty of spatulas. She never cooked a day in her life. But it sure made a spiffy impression whenever he came over and all the pots were in plain view on the stove or kitchen sink. See? Just when you thought that a naked woman soaking in a bubble bath was their ultimate fantasy, you realize . . . pots 'n' bubbles is just as good.

It is often said that men marry their mothers. But they don't necessarily want a woman wearing an apron and bonnet baking fluffy muffins in the kitchen. It has more to do with "mother knowing best." In other words, they want a competent woman who can think for herself, handle her business, take charge, and tell him to knock off the foolishness—just like Mommy did when he was growing up.

When he's trying to make you jealous, he wants to see who is behind the wheel. When his little plan swirls out of control and he sees you take an unexpected detour, he pulls up the emergency brake and repositions himself. Then he begins to obey the driving rules, and from then on he drives like he has good sense.

Sophie was dating Tyler and they were in a committed relationship. Tyler told her about a female friend who, according to him, "wanted him." (Again, he's announcing it. It's obvious. That means she has nothing to worry about.) Sophie read the situation and responded calmly: "I don't want to interfere, and I wouldn't want you to make the wrong decision. If you want to see other people, that's fine. See if you like her and let me know when you've made your decision." Sophie hung up the phone, and the next day Tyler sent roses to her work. When she called to thank him, he invited her to go away for the weekend to a romantic hotel in Santa Barbara. The mystery woman's name never came up again.

If you don't react, guess what? Oops. The button has been permanently disconnected, and is no longer fun to push. If he continues to make innocent references to a particular ex-girlfriend repeatedly, all you have to do is put the shoe on the other foot. "Luke used to make me laugh all the time. And my folks just loved Luke." He will never see another *Star Wars* movie without cringing at the name Luke.

RELATIONSHIP PRINCIPLE 44

Once *you* start doing the same thing *he* was doing, suddenly, the bad behavior will magically disappear.

If you put the shoe on the other foot, does this mean you were "playing games"? Absolutely not. It was *his* game to begin with. He dragged you into it, kicking and screaming. He ran to first base, stole second, and rounded third. (You simply finished the game and brought him home.)

Female Button 2: He may forget to call, come in late, or pull back in some way.

Men are used to having the upper hand. When a man becomes a little standoffish, he's watching to see how persistent you'll become. Just like women play hard to get, men do the same. If he gets any inkling that you're willing to follow him around like a puppy, his next move may be to see if you'll "work for it" like a puppy jumping for a biscuit. (You have to let him know that your middle name ain't Sparky.)

That said, he *should* feel desired. He should feel valued, appreciated, and adored. Just not after he behaves badly; otherwise you'll create a monster.

A perfect example is Thomas, who was used to getting a reaction from Faith after staying out late drinking with the boys. Faith asked him numerous times to call when he was out late. He didn't. This went on for a year. One Friday night he tiptoed in at

4:00 A.M., went to the refrigerator, and poured a couple of beers down the sink so it would look like he had come home earlier. After staging the crime scene with the empty bottles, he crashed on the couch. When he awoke Saturday morning, Faith was gone. A girlfriend who is a flight attendant called Faith and asked her if she'd like to hop a flight to Hawaii for the weekend. Thomas didn't know, and for the rest of the weekend he freaked out, panicked, and called her friends and family to locate Faith.

(Fast forward a day and a half.) Sunday night, Faith comes bouncing in with a tan, the smell of coconut oil, and a gorgeous lei around her neck. "Aloha!" Suddenly, there was a complete role reversal. "Why didn't you call? I was worried sick!" Then came a lecture about being more considerate. Faith listened while munching on Hawaiian Mauna Loa nuts. Then she responded, "I don't understand why you are giving me such a hard time. Didn't I bring you back some nuts? Besides, if you total up the hours you've stayed out late drinking in the past year, it wouldn't even be a fraction of the hours I was gone." Then she pranced upstairs to unpack. Thomas never forgot to call Faith again. He went out half as often, came in at a decent hour, and even bought her a fancy cell phone so they could always reach each other.

RELATIONSHIP PRINCIPLE 45

When a man doesn't call, a bunch of scenarios will typically run through a woman's mind. Similarly, his imagination will run wild when he doesn't hear from you.

If you can't afford a trip to Hawaii and don't know any flight attendants, there is another, far less expensive alternative to deal with the "partner rolls in just before dawn" dilemma. There is a new invention that is sold at Home Depot or any hardware store commonly referred to as a dead bolt. (When used once in very cold temperatures, it has a 99 percent effectiveness rate.)

When a man is coming in late or he doesn't call, he's in control. Some even play up the party-boy façade: "Oh, man, I am so hung over. We had so many mai tais last night." He probably had beer nuts, a stolen green olive from the bar, and one light beer. "If I stay out all night drinking, will she leave tread marks in the carpet from pacing back and forth?" So he'll act like he's a beer-drinking pig . . . and damn proud of it. Why? Because when he knows someone is waiting, worried and upset, he feels cared about. It's the same feeling you get when he sends roses, a limo, and tickets to the theater.

Even teenage boys do this with their mothers. Stevie, age thirteen, said, "If I know my mommy is going to yell at me, I may as well stay out at the arcade even later, and have another soda pop. If you call while you are out, you know you are going to get yelled at anyway. So why spoil all the fun? You may as well just get yelled at once when you get home, instead of getting yelled at twice."

On the other hand, if he comes home and you aren't even there for his grand entrance, it's no fun anymore. "Where is she? I didn't get my adrenaline kick. Wait, she doesn't care where I am or where I've been. Why *isn't* she upset?" I've even heard some men come right out and say, "I stay out late because it makes my girlfriend appreciate me more." (Her reaction reassures him she cares.)

As common as the "drinking late" scenario is the "working late" scenario. Brett was dating Andrea for a short while. He called and said he was thinking of canceling because of a grueling day at the office. It was left that he wanted to "play it by ear." When Brett called back at five o'clock, he had a second wind and wanted to get together, but Andrea had already made other plans. She then used the magic words: "I didn't want to make you feel any pressure. So, I made plans to go to a barbecue."

Remember this magic phrase: *I don't want you to feel any pressure.* It works like a charm with men who work really hard at their careers. Successful men explained that they are constantly fielding demands to do things out of obligation, pressure, and commitment to work.

The last thing he needs when he's Donald Trumpin' is a lover who gives him more of the same. Be the exception to the rule.

If he has a legitimate reason for not calling, be understanding. If you do address it, the best thing you can do is be direct, use reasoning, and keep your response measured. This shows self-control. If a guy is late a couple of times, in a matter-of-fact tone say, "I noticed you're always late. So if we make a date, and you're not here by eight thirty, I'm going to run over to my favorite Pilates class that starts at eight thirty. At the very least, give me a heads-up so I don't miss you." This is called a "truthful untruth." You are saying "give me a heads-up" instead of "call me" and telling him that you will make other plans if he keeps you hanging. The casual approach takes the "stink" off of it. Translation? Self-control.

RELATIONSHIP PRINCIPLE 46

The more rational and calm you remain, the more emotional he will become.

And keep your radar antenna pulled up. If he says, "I lost track of time with the boys," or, "I completely forgot," that should signal your radar that he's doing it to get attention. If you give him some, he'll do it again, so act like you didn't even notice. The only time you *should* address it is if you had tentative plans and he held you up by not calling. Then lower the boom. How? With men, don't start with a long story that leads up to what you are going to say. That tells him you are unsure of yourself. Instead, just call it . . . fix it . . . and get over it.

1. **Call it.** "In the future, don't leave me hanging. My time is valuable to me, and there were a lot of other plans I could have made."	**Between the lines:** Note that you said *your* time is valuable. You aren't necessarily indicating your time *with him* is valuable.
2. **Fix it.** "Please give me the same courtesy that you would give to a client you work with."	**Between the lines:** You are equating the situation to a work example. (Lo and behold, a logical woman.)
3. **Get over it.** Now drop the subject like it never came up.	**Between the lines:** Translation: The negotiations are now over.

What a lot of men infer is that when you drop hints or beat around the bush, you don't feel comfortable enough with yourself or the communication in the relationship to speak your mind. When you state your case in two sentences, *and then drop it*, it demonstrates confidence. "Uh-oh. If I try that again, it will get me replaced." It makes him consider commitment much more strongly when he sees that you can't be trifled with.

RELATIONSHIP PRINCIPLE 47

To a man, it is totally inappropriate to be emotional when talking about something important. When you speak calmly, he assumes it's much more important.

The first thing he will hear is *your tone of voice*, and only then will he give clout or credibility *to the content* of what you are saying. If your voice is supercharged with emotion, he will assume that even you don't know what is wrong. "She's emotional, so I'm just going to tune her out." Then he will hit the Mute button and tune you out. "She's under my thumb. I can do whatever I want and she'll still be there." Therefore, if you want him to hear you, you have to be very matter-of-fact.

The first thing a true fighter learns is that one must pick one's battles wisely. A champion fighter won't stand there swinging hard and slugging it out with a ninety-pound weakling. A good fighter knows that if he fights every battle, even if they are strong ones, he'll start losing because of battle fatigue.

So a way to avert a fight is to call him out, in one sentence or less.

In a matter-of-fact tone say,
"This is unnecessary, wouldn't you agree?"

Or you can ask in the form of a question. Tilt your head and ever-so-casually ask,
"Is this something you think is normal?"

If he asks you what you are talking about, simply rephrase it.
"Is this something you regularly do? I was just wondering."

Then be silent. If he gives you a response that doesn't fly, say,
"I see."

Then nod, take a sip of your cocktail, and change the subject.

Notice how you *aren't* being pulled in, but at the same time you are signaling that his behavior is unacceptable. Whenever you take the high road, others are quicker to feel low. When you don't give him a negative reaction, you aren't giving him anything to assuage his guilt. He can't put the "crazy mark" on you. He can't say, "She's a live wire. Look at her. She's attacking me for no good reason." That gives him an out, so he never has to examine his own behavior. *Or correct it.*

This reminds me of the motto from the movie *Primary Colors*, in which John Travolta plays a satiric version of former President Clinton. When he is asked why he won't do attack ads against his opponent and run a negative campaign, he quips, "I just don't want to give that son of a bitch the power to make *me* the son of a bitch."

Whenever you sense you are being pulled in, remember this saying: "Never wrestle with a pig. If you do, you'll both get filthy. But the difference is *the pig will love it.*"

Female Button 3: He may say something off-color to see how you respond.

Part of testing is finding out where *your* unique buttons are. (Inquiring egos want to know.) So a man might put his boots up on your coffee table. He may use your pretty Ralph Lauren bathroom towel with the decorative pink bow on it to mop up around the toilet after he "sprays." As he grows more comfortable, he may emit a deadly plume of toxic or lethal fumes after eating chili. Or he may say something a little outrageous or off-color, like ask you to come over in a trench coat and high heels, to see how you'll react. It's all by design to see how you come at him.

One guy even admitted, "I sometimes say things to piss my girlfriend off because she looks so sexy when she's annoyed."

To show you how commonplace in the male "school of thought" that it is perfectly acceptable to deliberately provoke someone (even if you like him), I have excerpted a classic example from one of Donald Trump's books, *Trump: How to Get Rich*. Not only does he admit he tries to rile people, he advises his readers to do the same. Why? "To see what the reaction is." Here's what he says:

> *If you say something seemingly off the cuff, you may get a revealing response. I might make an outrageous comment in a meeting just to see whether the other people play along or take a stand and disagree. It's a good way of assessing the mettle of the folks across the table. Do they want to be liked? Are they comfortable with unpredictability? Are they capable of candor?*

Men do this all the time to get you to drop the "nice" veil, so they can see how you scrap. It's a little like what a carnivorous animal does when it's curious. It's called "gumming." A bear will break into a car and then gently nibble on a small object to see what it is. Is it an animal? Is it still alive? Is it edible? What texture does it have? The bite is not a death blow. The bear just shakes it around a little and gives it a little nibble.

Where do men learn this? Let us now explore the origins of this learned behavior by "getting in touch with his inner seventh-grader."

When a young boy is growing up, chances are he played a game on the playground called The Dozens. Basically, several boys gather around and begin to bag on one another. They exchange verbal potshots with precision:

Boy 1: "Your mom has an ass that's so big, it covers two whole zip codes."

Boy 2: "You don't look anything like your daddy."

Boy 3: "Your auntie has a flat face like a Pekingese dog."

If one of the little boys loses his cool or shows any sign of crying, whimpering, or cracking under pressure, *he gets kicked out of the game.* So they learn: Vulnerability equals hell. This game is also called Lemon Squeezer because a kid might want to cry but can't. So his facial expression will look like he just bit into a lemon because he's wincing and fighting back the tears. The winner is the little boy who kept his cool and had the most convincing comebacks. This is how men learn to trade verbal blows.

Adult men playfully abuse one another the very same way. They see it as emotional toughening and a male form of affection. If one guy shed a tear in 1986 because his team lost the playoffs, he'll never live it down at the weekly poker game.

"Hey, Bobby? I bought you a box of Kleenex tissues with your name on it. It's in the powder room. Help yourself."

"Bobby, get me a beer from the kitchen while you are up. Don't forget my doily. Bobby likes being the bitch in the relationship."

"Bobby has a nice ass. Wouldn't he look good in a push-up bra?"

This is where his jokes come from when he roughhouses with you. It's actually endearing. It's his way of telling you he sees you as an equal. They think of it as a playful way of "romantically sparring with you." One guy explained, "You want a woman who'll joke around and be your partner in crime. No guy wants a yes-girl." He's looking to see if you'll be able to stand up for yourself *without falling apart*. If you can give it right back, he'll see you as a trusted partner. "This one is well rounded."

RELATIONSHIP PRINCIPLE 48

Many men reduce women to a set of givens. A man relies on the fact that most women are emotional and that he'll be able to push your emotional buttons once he finds out where they are. When he can't, he'll often crumble and become the more vulnerable one in the relationship.

Men assume women simply cannot be analytical, and that we are "technically challenged" in the sciences. I recall overhearing a few guys watching a news program that featured a female astronaut on a NASA space mission. One guy looked so spooked, the other guy began to console him. "Look, someone's gotta to do the cookin' and washin' up there in space."

Men banter and say things in jest about women being in the police force too. And the military. Why? Women are too emotional, and emotional creatures can't be fully armed. When the platoon goes out commando style, men are afraid that the girlie in the unit will get scared, cry, panic and empty her automatic weapon in the wrong direction—and accidentally mow down half her platoon. If they could turn back the clocks, they would. All the women would have to turn in their rifles and get certified to carry vegetable peelers. During the dedication ceremony, you'd hear the trumpets play and the soldiers would be honored with Purple Heart pins. Then the "little ladies" would get little purple pots. "We hereby honor you for whipping up a great snack in the face of incoming mortars."

So men tend to be a little predisposed. And when you surprise him with a reasoned approach, he'll think, "This one's got fire. She's a keeper." A lot of women don't realize that showing you have a brain and a mind of your own is often the way to win his trust and respect.

RELATIONSHIP PRINCIPLE 49

He is testing to see if you believe in yourself. He wants to know who is at the controls. When you aren't easily shaken he sees, "This one can't be manipulated."

A girlfriend named Renee has a great comeback she always uses with her boyfriend. Sometimes, he'll call her in a crabby mood. To avert a spat, she'll end the conversation in a cute way. She'll say, "Have you eaten? You sound hungry. Go eat something, and don't call me back until you have a full belly." It's sort of like the one where men say, "Are you having PMS?" Only it's affectionate rather than insulting. And, the best part is that it can be used as a defense to his crabbiness during breakfast, lunch, dinner, and every hour in between.

A guy named Harold talked about what he finds irresistible in his feisty fiancée. "When I harass my fiancée verbally, she'll put me in my place." They were talking about marriage and he said, "Why buy the cow when you can get the milk for free?" Instead of getting defensive, his fiancée Robyn, laughed and came back with, "I know what you mean. Why buy the pig when all you want is a little sausage?"

Before he'll go on a roped bridge to cross from one mountaintop to another, he'll shake it to see how secure it is or whether it will fall apart. Men will watch to see how you do battle. "Is she a warrior? Or will she be din-din? Before he becomes your knight in shining armor he wants to know, "Is she even worth defending?"

Female Button 4: He may push the envelope to see how much he can get away with.

A happily married woman of thirty-five years told me a story about her husband. When they were newlyweds, her husband would leave sopping wet towels everywhere. On the bed, on the floor, over the doors—you name it, there was a towel on it. When asking him to pick up his towels didn't work, she started throwing them out the second-floor window onto the "towel tree." Before every shower, he would go outside and pick a towel off his tree. Summer turned to winter and the towels were losing their "effervescent smell." And that's when he decided to comply with the U.N. household resolutions. (If it isn't in the hamper it does not get washed.)

What some men do is pretend they are incapable of doing something, so you'll always get stuck doing it. My girlfriend Julie is a good example of this. Her husband dressed their daughter in a green shirt, yellow shorts, and red socks. Julie wanted to say, "Are you color blind? She looks like Bozo!" But instead she said, "Oh, honey, thanks for getting the baby dressed while I showered. That was so thoughtful." Then she did a little damage control and changed the baby's socks while Big Daddy started the car.

Men do it all the time. They feign incompetence. They'll deliberately do a horrible job on the dishes, the laundry, and the ironing—to avoid being asked to do it again. If you criticize him about any domestic duties, parenting things, or stereotypically female chores, he'll say, "Fine. If I don't know what to do, then you do it." This is precisely the scenario you want to avoid because from then on, you'll get stuck doing it.

RELATIONSHIP PRINCIPLE 50

To encourage the right behavior, state what you want, and then give him the solution. Show him how he can be your hero.

Paulette did this with her husband, to a tee. She and her husband both work full-time. They have an understanding that whoever gets home first is the one who starts cooking dinner. Paulette said, "Whenever I pull up and I see he's not home, I keep driving and stay gone long enough for him to get the food ready. I pick up dessert, and then I rave about how good his cooking is. Now he does all the cooking."

If you want him to do the grocery shopping, appeal to his ego. Say, "I don't know what you like. And you are so much better at it than I am. You should go. Here's my list. . . ." When he gets back, tell him, "You are definitely the expert with this. Nobody does it better."

Strategic helplessness can be very *helpful*, indeed. Animals use similar diversionary tactics in the wild. When a mama duck has a brood of baby ducks and a predator is around, the duck creates a distraction by pretending to be wounded and flapping around everywhere. She steers the predator's attention away from the babies. And as soon as he's been lured far enough away from the little ones, she flies back to them.

The Buttons on His Remote Control

Another rule of thumb when communicating with men: You should never say, "Honey, we need to talk." He will run for the hills like there's a hurricane warning.

Warning: *A flurry of feelings ahead.*

Outlook: *Not so good.*

Tonight's forecast: *Flannel muumuus, turbulence, and unexplained headaches in the bedroom.*

Pop psychologists tell you that if you don't want someone to feel attacked when you address a conflict, you should begin every sentence with "I *feel* . . ." rather than "You . . . ," With the male species, it pushes the right buttons a lot quicker if you leave feelings out of it and tell him what you *think*. When in Rome . . . talk like Romeo. Romeo would begin sentences with:

"I believe . . ."

"By my estimation . . ."

"My take is . . ."

"How I analyze the situation is . . ."

"Objectively speaking . . ."

You will get his immediate attention when you use non-emotional words (which he is completely unprepared for). Following are the seven words men love to use, interchangeably. I've included a quick-reference guide to the male definitions of these words.

A CRASH COURSE IN MALE-SPEAK

LOGICAL

Used when he endearingly describes you to all his buddies, over a few beers: "She is uncontrollable. Luckily for her, I am logical."

SENSIBLE

Sensible is another favorite. Men think women aren't sensible because they buy a lot of shoes and expensive handbags to impress other women. Men, on the other hand, are sensible. For example, he thinks it is "sensible" to buy a forty-thousand-dollar studded motorcycle, so that he can enjoy the benefits of internal bleeding (and irreversible hearing loss) while riding in style. It's even better when he's wearing two thousand dollars' worth of Harley leather clothing so he can look stylish wearing that neck brace in the ambulance.

PRACTICAL

Men think that home items like throw pillows or decorative towels in the bathroom are ridiculous and "impractical." Curtains are impractical. Practical is what he insists he is being when he hangs up a Mexican serape from Tijuana in lieu of a curtain and then refers to it as "mood lighting." After all, nothing screams "do me" like a scratchy blanket covered in dog hair.

STRATEGIC

Men love the word *strategic*. "Since we both work, I think it would be a good move strategically if we employed a maid." The word *strategic* makes him feel like he is an important businessman, like he is El Presidente of the household. Not only this, it stirs up fond, soothing memories of when they were children playing with their miniature soldiers.

ANALYTICAL

An ability bestowed only upon the male species, to "analyze" how women are too emotional.

REASONABLE

His opinion.

UNREASONABLE

Your opinion.

Our male-speak class is now adjourned, but before you go, remember your homework assignment. Instead of "We need to talk about my feelings," say, "Let's analyze the situation *rationally* and *logically*." Now you are the one holding the remote and pushing all the buttons.

The first thing that will happen is that he will turn and look at you. Then he will look confused. He may look down to see if you are still genetically female. Then the lights will go on. Not only will it impress him, it will even make you look like you know what you are talking about. As for the look on his face? Priceless.

5

WANTED:

JOE PAYCHECK

Why Financial Independence Makes You Desirable as a Wife

I like compliments. But I prefer cash.

~ANONYMOUS

The Captain of My Gravy Train

There are certain things a man who is dating you will not come out and say. First and foremost, a man won't tell you that he's scared of having his clock cleaned in a divorce. Or that he's horrified of being stuck in a marriage with a woman who makes him feel like an ATM machine. Or that he is valued only because of what he can provide. To a man, that is the worst kind of entrapment.

When my editor Amanda Murray asked me what the subtitle of this book should be, I asked a couple of men for their input. One guy jokingly said, "It should be called *Why Men Marry Bitches: A Woman's Guide to Early Retirement*." Funny though it is, it speaks to the heart of what men fear most: a woman who is marrying because of her "business acumen." Not because of true love.

RELATIONSHIP PRINCIPLE 51

When he's dating you, he'll constantly be on guard and watching to discern, "Does she like me for who I am? Or for what I can provide?"

When a man takes a bitchier, independent woman out to dinner, he's not thinking to himself, "Without me, she won't eat." If he takes her away for the weekend and he's discussing the $1.6 million real estate deal he closed, her response will be, "Good for you. Congratulations." But she won't seem terribly impressed or hungry to get a piece of it. If he picks her up in a $350,000 Aston Martin, she'll get into the car and say, "Thank you for picking me up. It was thoughtful of you to drive so far out of your way." *This shows that she appreciates him, not the car.* This is the woman who will make a man get out of his "me, myself, and I" mode and get him thinking in "we" mode. Why? Because she is *unimpressed* by the shallow things most women are impressed by. This sets her apart.

It's your independence that wins his heart. He marries the woman who lets him know she'd sooner be picked up in a used Dodge with dents in the side and hubcaps missing, than to be treated with disrespect. If he has a bad attitude or isn't a gentleman, he has to know you will hail a cab or take the bus home. It's when he feels you can't be "bought" that he thinks about marriage.

When it comes to marriage, men tend to shy away from women who know all the expensive hot spots. Or a woman who name-drops, and is all too familiar with accoutrements of success. When she says, "Nice Rolex!" what he sees is a potential shakedown on his horizon.

Ever seen those want-ads where a woman places an ad looking for a "generous man" to "take care of her"? What the guy's read is, "I'm selling myself like a used Buick with a bad transmission." It doesn't matter what else that ad says. She can talk about walks on the beach until the cows come home. All he'll see is a financial agenda. Here's what he'll interpret when reading between the lines:

WANTED: JOE PAYCHECK

Do you have a house I can take? Are you plenty happy being a working fool and handing over all your money? If so, I've got a prize package for you featuring three interest-earning babies so I can expand my retirement portfolio. If you call now, I promise to tell all my girlfriends you're hung like a three-hundred-pound llama, even if you are hung like a light switch. Plus, I'll even convert to make the in-laws happy. I am an equal opportunist. So hurry, I'll be standing by with all my bonbons.

A quality guy won't say, "Gee, where do I sign up for that?" Remember, bitch stands for **B**abe **I**n **T**otal **C**ontrol of **H**erself. It doesn't stand for **B**ecause **I** **T**ook **C**harlie's **H**ouse.

RELATIONSHIP PRINCIPLE 52

When a man sees you are focused on your own dreams or on elevating yourself, he feels safer marrying you because he doesn't worry about what you'll be trying to take away *from him.*

Men, more than ever, are warming up to the idea that a woman who can contribute financially can be an important asset. He marries a woman who has depth. Men worry about making ends meet and what you would do if he fell short of cash.

Men are secretly afraid of being inadequate and of showing their weak side. They are afraid that after they woo you, and they turn out to be less than the Prince Charming fantasy you fell in love with, you'll up and split. Rest assured, men have dreams of finding that special girl to spend the rest of their lives with. But in his dreams, his partner is someone *he can count on*. This is why a bitch appeals to men. She's more real, she doesn't buy into his BS. She's less likely to bolt when he drops his veil.

Men don't talk about this need for "security" because it's not considered manly. It's taboo. But they want the feeling of security also. Here's what runs through his mind when he thinks about marrying you:

"Would she grab the next available cash cow
if I was struggling financially?"

"Would she be able to hold down the fort
if there was an emergency?"*

"Would she leave me for a guy with
a new Mercedes and a bigger house?"

*This one is a biggie.

Men tend to approach love as though it's a business-deal negotiation. One of the most common things I heard in my interviews with men was the question, "What is she bringing to the table other than sex?" Here's where the bitch quotient comes in again. Men usually label a weaker woman as a liability and a stronger woman as an asset. It's just like business school when there is an acquisition and they calculate the "value added." His knee-jerk observation goes something like this:

LIABILITY:	ASSET:
A woman who is desperately looking for a guy to rescue her from her life. Her only goal is, "I need a boyfriend." "It will be like adopting a child I'll need to take care of. She needs someone to pay the bills."	A strong woman with goals, who won't give herself away. Then he feels, "She really loves me for who I am. She's not with me because she needs a meal ticket or a daddy."

As Will Smith said, "Competence is the thing that is most attractive." Men regularly said the same thing: They want a woman who can TCB (**T**ake **C**are of **B**usiness). It turns them on mentally and sexually also. It gives him something men aren't supposed to need: a feeling of protection and safety.

When he meets a woman who can buy her own cup of coffee, she exudes a do-it-yourself attitude that immediately earns his respect. Men are drawn to women who see themselves as winners.

Peter recalled his early impressions of his wife, Kim. "She was a native-born Chinese woman who came here from another country and didn't even speak the language. She started her own business and became successful. And that's pretty amazing, considering the fact that she didn't speak a word of English when she arrived." I asked him if Kim's traditional upbringing made her submissive in their relationship. "Oh, hell no. She doesn't put up with any crap from me. Not for a second." Notice what he respects: Kim's strength of character. The only time she'll take a handout is when it's coming from her *other* hand.

Now compare this to a woman who isn't building anything other than a wardrobe, and comes into a relationship with a sense of entitlement. She is pretty, but then she starts talking about her "goddess" energy or her "diva-like" qualities. Or she'll use the word *queen*: "I am a queen. Any man of mine has to *worship* the ground I walk on. And he has to worship my dog Princess too." Then she orders the most expensive thing on the menu because "she's worth it" and poses on a barstool as if she's Queen Elizabeth having her portrait painted. All of which comes back to bite her in his exit speech. "Dating me is not going to be fair to you. As a goddess, you deserve so much more. I can't treat you the way you deserve to be treated and I would hate to see you suffer. I think we need to take a break from dating."

A friend of mine named Bobby said, "Sometimes you feel like you want to ask a girl, 'Hey, uh, could you bring your credit-card statements to our next date? I want to know what kind of *lifestyle you've become accustomed to* before things get too serious. Are you a cash burner? Do you spend three times what you make?'"

RELATIONSHIP PRINCIPLE 53

Men don't judge how much money you have.

They notice *how you budget*

what you do have.

As early as the first date, he'll be imagining what his life would be like if he stepped inside your world. So he'll start fact gathering and recording everything in his memory banklike a video camera with two legs. Here's what he'll record:

The Marriage "Risk Assessment"

Things men notice:

- ✓ If you carry a three-thousand-dollar designer purse (with fifty cents inside).
- ✓ If you have a new car that is all scraped up and looks like a rolling storage unit.
- ✓ If your place is clean and inviting or unkempt (he'll assume that's what he'll come home to every day).
- ✓ If you have a huge stack of old bills on the countertop.
- ✓ If you have knobs missing off the TV or stereo (he'll assume you break things).
- ✓ Whether your animals are well taken care of.
- ✓ Whether you have a rotation of roommates who don't stick around very long (this means you are hard to live with).
- ✓ If the electricity or phone gets turned off (he infers he'll be adopting a young girl who will constantly need to be taken care of).
- ✓ If you are paying the cell bill with a maxed-out credit card and the collection agents are knocking at your door (you'll screw up his credit).

- ✓ If you have a closet crammed with shoes and clothes and tons of makeup scattered everywhere in the bathroom (your appearance is all you have to offer).
- ✓ If you don't return videos on time, or if you bounce checks.
- ✓ If you keep a well-stocked bar but have no food in the refrigerator (you might be a party girl, and not really suitable to live with).
- ✓ If you borrow money, or use the word help and have to rely on friends or family to make ends meet.
- ✓ If you've been married before and made out like a bandit in the divorce (he'll be worried that he's about to get dusted off as well).

Why these signals make or break your marriage potential

- These are clues that tell him whether you can build a life together. He's looking for signs of neglect because he wants to see how you'll treat the things he will work hard to provide. He won't comment on it, bring your attention to it, or break up over it. But he'll store everything in his memory and weigh the information *heavily* when deciding to move forward with marriage.

Most women think they have to worry about the guy's finances because he's the so-called provider. But today more than ever, men are looking at your finances also. Yes, even the wealthy ones.

The *Leave It to Beaver* standards have changed because of how much the cost of living has gone up. Back in the 1950s or 1960s, a Cadillac cost five thousand dollars and a home cost fifty thousand. Times are different. Now that same Cadillac costs fifty thousand and a house in a metropolitan area can easily be a half a million to a million, or more.

A really successful man named Kenny explained: "Women are taught they just have to be pretty, and a guy will take care of them. I've known women who made very little money, and lived in one-room apartments. But every time a bill needed to be sent out, it was sent out on time. She managed with what she had. She didn't dig herself into a hole. I've also known women who had a lot of money, but spent it on nonsense like two-hundred-dollar face creams with fetus protein in it, or a five-hundred-dollar dress. Two weeks later she cried because the electricity was turned off. Or she ran out of gas with her BMW, and had to walk to the gas station in a Chanel outfit. Then she acted like the whole world was picking on her. That's the type of woman who will put you in an early grave."

RELATIONSHIP PRINCIPLE 54

Men admire women who want to elevate themselves and pull themselves up by their own bootstraps, and fear women who are social climbers at a man's expense.

It can often be the reason he'll call off a wedding. Lee and Tracy are a perfect example of this. She was a hairstylist living with a roommate, and Lee was a very successful entrepreneur. She had dreams of owning her own salon, and Lee admired that. After nine months they got engaged, and he gave her a gorgeous canary diamond engagement ring. He also told her he'd pay for the wedding. She chose the Ritz-Carlton, a ten-thousand-dollar Vera Wang gown, and Tiffany's for the wedding registry. All the guests would be treated to a night at the Ritz with a complimentary facial or back massage (on his dime). The only thing that he told her he objected to was the Tiffany registry because he worried his working-class relatives wouldn't be able to afford the high-ticket gift items on her list.

Lee recalled, "I couldn't get my mind wrapped around why anyone would need to register for a nine-hundred-dollar Tiffany crystal punch bowl. I started to feel uneasy and it made me question the situation I was about to step into. When she quit her job, I realized I was making a huge mistake and broke off the engagement. I didn't feel like the wedding was about a true blue 'love thing' and that we'd be taking on the world together through thick and thin. It became about putting on a show for all her friends. It wasn't a life together that she wanted to build. It was a fairy tale she wanted me to pay for."

Since men don't usually share the Cinderella wedding fantasy, try to be mindful of how your anticipation looks to a guy. Men notice when a woman who has nothing of her own suddenly develops very expensive taste.

If you aren't self-sufficient (or *working* toward being self-sufficient), everything you say about commitment and marriage will be looked at with suspicion.

SHE ASKS:	HE HEARS:
"What are we doing for the holidays?"	"I can't wait to meet my new in-laws!
"Do you own a home?"	"I want to give a thirty-day notice and move in."
"Can I borrow your car?"	"Can I drive my new car?"
"Do you ever think about getting married?"	"I can't wait to quit my job."
"What are your intentions?"	"Where's my ring?"
"I refuse to waste my time."	"I bought the dress. Time's up. Let's set a date!"

This is what frustrates men, because they rarely hear a woman say, "I can't wait to start a business." Or, "I can't wait to take that real-estate class." With most women, their goals are, "I want to be married within one year." So she goes to the gym, buys makeup, looks fabulous, and doesn't understand why the relationship isn't moving forward.

Remember the classic scene from *My Cousin Vinny*? Marisa Tomei's character asks Vinny when they are going to get married: "My clock is ticking like this . . . [*stomp, stomp, stomp*]." It was great in the movie, but in real life this is the last thing he wants: a woman who is stomping her feet and who is pissed off because she can't believe she is being cheated out of the marriage she's *owed*. Men are so frustrated by this, they even have slang phrases they use with one another describe it.

"On a mission." Defined as any woman who wants to fall in love with a beautiful wedding, and isn't nearly as concerned about whether she's in love with the groom.

"Filling a position." The feeling he gets when he realizes her interest in marriage has nothing to do with him.

This is why you instantly become the one who is "different from all the rest" when you don't act like marriage is the holy grail.

The whole biological-clock thing is not just about babies. Women are socialized to believe that they have a shelf life, sexually. And, women buy into it. They don't see themselves as a prize after a certain age. When I spoke with men about the pressure on women to be married by a certain age, I was surprised to hear most men say this was a myth. If a woman takes care of herself, she can be sexy in her thirties, forties, fifties, and beyond. There is no "shelf life" for marriage. According to men, what makes a woman less desirable is the insecurity surrounding her sexuality, not the lack of it. Or, when a woman thinks *the only thing she has to offer is sex.* If a woman is twenty years old, attractive, and has her whole life in front of her, but she thinks her only bargaining chip is "I have a nice rack" or "look how cute my butt looks in these jeans," she will quickly become boring. If that's all she has to offer, if she isn't competent, spicy, and independent, that's what will make her less desirable.

Whenever I met a happily married man, I always made a point of asking what it was that made his wife different. Michael shared the following story. "When I met my wife, she held a prestigious position with an ad agency. Then she lost her job. So she waited on tables until she found a replacement job. She never took the 'oh, poor pitiful me' attitude. She was realistic. The bills needed to be paid, and she grabbed the bull by the horns. I respected her because she rolled with life's punches. And I knew then I could build a life with her." He was won over by how she handled adversity. It was her character that won him over. Even when times were tough, she wanted to stand on her own two feet.

This affects how a husband treats a wife after they are married too. Eva is happily married, and until recently her husband was the breadwinner. When she wanted to buy something from the Home Shopping Network, she would ask her husband. Sometimes he'd say, "Let's wait a week," which sounds a lot like something you'd say to a child: "Wait until you save up your allowance and then I'll buy that for you." So one day, without asking "prior permission," she took the initiative and got a part-time job. Now, instead of "Can I buy this?" she walks in and says, "Honey, look what I bought." And a funny thing happened. Eva noticed her husband's passion went through the roof.

Men feel more emotionally connected to a woman who can be a little authoritative sometimes. The woman who can get up and leave at any time is the one who can put him in check. When a man meets a competent woman who doesn't need him, he instantly treats her *differently* than the woman who seems unsure of what she wants out of life. That's the woman he marries.

RELATIONSHIP PRINCIPLE 55

He doesn't want to marry a helpless little girl whom he will have to take care of.

The helpless or frail woman who can't make decisions will quickly turn him off in the bedroom also.

Although there is an exception to every rule. Once in a blue moon, you'll come across a guy who wants a helpless wife or a "little girl" who will stay in the kitchen and bake cookies. This is why some men get a mail-order bride. Of course, his drastic decision to marry a foreigner usually comes on the heels of a horrifying experience (like dating an American woman who used too many big words). So he swears off American women and runs off to a distant land to meet the bride of his dreams. (Just as soon as he's done getting a few hair plugs put in.) And it is pure bliss, just like they promised in the . . .

Mail-Order Bride Catalog

Your Blushing Bride Comes with the Following Tender Moments . . .

She doesn't speak a word of English. Therefore, she will never voice an opinion or disagree. She will simply give you dirty looks and use expletives in her native tongue when you don't allow her to go to the prom.

If you have TiVo, you can eliminate the horrible documentaries about the "Women's Movement" and show her the finer things in life: Shake 'n Bake.

The vows will be nondenominational. "Do you promise to obey . . . and obey . . . and obey, until immigration status do you part?"

At the reception, we'll provide a rum cake for all the adults. We'll also provide Puddin' Pops for the bride and her classmates.

We'll even give you a sentimental gift, gratis, from our wedding registry. You can choose from either a harness, a swing, or a swatting paddle for the honeymoon in Hoboken, New Jersey.

It's true. You never hear about a messy divorce with a mail-order bride. She stays until the green card comes. After that, she goes to the market to buy a quart of milk and is never seen or heard from again. *Poof!* She disappears into thin air like a mafia turncoat entering a witness protection program.

Obviously, men who mail-order brides are taking advantage of these women's economic situation. But this is the exception, not the rule. Men don't want a helpless little Stepford Wife. If he has a lot going for him, he wants a partner who will have his back. When he sees that a woman can make good decisions in her own life, he will instantly feel closer to her. "Cool. We are like-minded." That's the woman he'll take with him to pick out a starter home, new carpet, and new furniture. She becomes an asset. A man likes a woman who knows her own mind, who can think, especially if he trusts her. Because then a lot of pressure is lifted off him when he doesn't have to always make all the decisions.

RELATIONSHIP PRINCIPLE 56

For a man, the words *respect* and *trust* are interchangeable. If he doesn't respect you, he will not trust you. And without trust, he will always keep you at arm's length.

Appreciation: The Inroad to His Heart

More than food, more than sex—whether you make a man feel appreciated when you are seriously dating will often make or break whether he ties the knot. And that's another thing you never hear about in a woman's magazine. Appreciation is the way to a man's heart. He'll go to the ends of the earth just to have a woman make him feel adored. Mary Kay Ash said, "There are two things people want more than sex and money . . . recognition and praise."

Sometimes a guy will do something for you, like bring a gift, buy flowers, run errands with you, put gas in your car. When he does small things and you don't say, "That was so thoughtful. Thank you," he will start to give less. Eventually, whatever he gives will become mechanical—offered with little or no real feeling on his part. His feelings will wither away until he disconnects altogether.

This is why men stay late at work and avoid going home to their wives. It's why they stop making an effort. Nothing will demotivate him faster than feeling that he's unappreciated.

RELATIONSHIP PRINCIPLE 57

When he gives you something, always acknowledge the kindness behind the gesture, not the material item itself. Just like women can't get too many compliments, a man can't get too much appreciation for his contribution.

Danny told a story about a woman he had wined and dined for several months. One weekend, she invited him over for a steak dinner to reciprocate. When he got to her house and opened the fridge, he noticed there were two items inside: mustard and stale bread. Debra said, "I meant to get to the grocery store. Could we go to the market?" He accompanied her into the market and started pushing a cart for her. She grabbed a second cart and announced, "We're going to need both." She then proceeded to pack both carts to full-tilt capacity. The carts were so heavy that she could barely push hers through the checkout stand. The bill? Close to two hundred dollars.

Danny said, "I paid for it all, and she never thanked me or even acknowledged it. To top it off, she didn't even cook me a decent dinner. She opened a Value Pak and made me a four-ounce piece of chicken. [And Danny is a big guy.] The sixteen-ounce steaks I picked out mysteriously vanished." When I asked him if he ever took her out again, he said, "I'd sooner date a mugger who wore a ski mask and robbed me at gunpoint."

When I interviewed men, this was one of the biggest reasons that they had reservations about marriage. If you want to *talk a man out of* being generous, all you have to do is create the impression that what he just gave was consumed, vaporized, and absorbed with very little appreciation. It's the quickest way to take the fun out of his courting you. As one man put it, "Your days will be numbered."

RELATIONSHIP PRINCIPLE 58

A man's favorite word is *appreciate*.

He wants more than anything to feel revered and valued by a woman.

When she's appreciative, it motivates him to give her the world.

When you act like you appreciate his accomplishments, what he did for you, what he gave to you, and so on—this is the most important validation he can get. This explains why men will forget a birthday, an anniversary, and Mother's Day . . . but they'll never miss a "coach of the year" award ceremony to get that crummy little trophy cup.

He won't hand over his heart on a platter, buy a ring, pay for a wedding, and give you a house if you wolf down a dinner like it meant nothing to you. Therefore, if you want him to give you the stars, the sun, and the moon (and the pear-shaped diamond), be sure to say the magic words.

Acknowledge what he did and make a fuss over it.

"I appreciate your fixing [whatever he fixed]. It is so helpful."

"It was really fun the other night at [wherever he took you]. Thanks again."

"I absolutely love [a gift he gave you, even if you hated it]. Thank you again."

Then add:

"Thank you, that was so generous of you."

Or, "That was thoughtful of you."

There are no sweeter words to a man's ears.

Now let's look at the situation with the polar opposite: the guy who refuses to give. At the same time that you should acknowledge kindness and generosity, don't be too tolerant of a guy who is cheap. Beware of the guy who suffers from a disease called "tightwad-itis." It reveals his lack of interest in anything long-term.

For example, Samantha went on a date with a guy who was well off. We'll call him Squeaky. (As in, some guys are so tight they squeak when they walk.) Before the dinner, he took Samantha to an ATM on the way to the restaurant and made her wait in the car while he withdrew twenty bucks. After he got in the car, he put the twenty dollar bill on the dashboard as if to let her know, "This is all that's going to be spent." Then he took her to a hole-in-the-wall place ("Cheapskates Bar and Grill") and suggested that they share a greasy appetizer. They got out of there for just shy of twenty dollars including tip, and you could clearly see it was very unnerving and painful for him. He practically needed 3-in-l oil to help get his wallet open.

This is the date you want to cut short. Do the math. Twenty dollars should have lasted roughly forty-five minutes. That's one dollar for every two minutes with five extra courtesy minutes for the "just friends" speech. ("Just friends" is code for "no sex.") If he takes it hard, add two minutes for pity time, and then ske-daddle.

RELATIONSHIP PRINCIPLE 59

A man will not be thinking about how much he spends on you if he believes you could be "the one." In the beginning, he will be *happy* to pick up the tab.

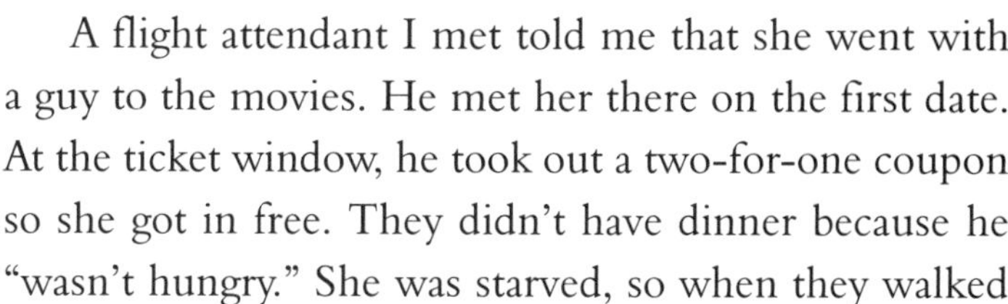

A flight attendant I met told me that she went with a guy to the movies. He met her there on the first date. At the ticket window, he took out a two-for-one coupon so she got in free. They didn't have dinner because he "wasn't hungry." She was starved, so when they walked by the concession stand she said she wanted a hot dog. He said to her, "Let's go get our seats first, then we'll get food." They got their seats, and he stayed seated. So she got up and said, "I'm going to get a hot dog. Would you like anything?" He said, "Okay. I'll have a large Coke. Wait . . . ." When he opened his wallet, she thought he was going to take out a $20 bill. Instead, he took out a coupon that said ONE FREE 32-OUNCE COKE and gave it to her.

Not that this is a bad arrangement, necessarily. It's wonderful to have platonic friends you can go to the movies with, especially if they are gay. (At least then, you may get some good fashion and makeup tips.)

A girlfriend of mine named Chloe was invited on a first date to a baseball game with a guy named Joe. After the game, they were in his car and he asked for reimbursement of her ticket. She said she didn't have money, so he said she could send a check. "Your ticket was thirty-six dollars. Just give me forty, and that will include the gas. I'll pay for the hot dogs and nachos." She said, "Um, you invited me, so I didn't come prepared with any money." He said, "Aw, hey. No problem. Just pay me next week sometime."

The following week, Joe called and left his address on her voice mail. She returned his call and said, "I'm sending a check. But I'm deducting money for this phone call, postage, and money for the envelope. Since you're such a tightwad, I won't charge you for my ink. But only if you promise never to call here again."

RELATIONSHIP PRINCIPLE 60

A man who is financially comfortable but still very stingy doesn't want to give—*anything*. He won't want to be inconvenienced with his time, with sharing a dresser—much less a home or a life together.

After all, partnership is about sharing your life together. A man who feels he may have met his soul mate will not be that obsessed with what he spends, as long as he thinks you aren't taking advantage of him. If he likes you, the only thing he'll care about is getting your affections. As one man explained, "It's a good feeling to a guy to be the generous one, and to be able to take a woman out when you are in love with her."

Coupons, refunds, splitting plates, or a severe reluctance to pick up the tab—all of these should not go unnoticed, because he's showing you he doesn't really take the relationship seriously. As one man explained, "A guy cannot be madly in love with you and be really cheap at the same time." And if he is just a cheap bastard? You wouldn't want to be with him anyway. Imagine what those wedding vows would sound like. (A trailer-trash moment to behold.) "I promise to love and honor . . .

in sickness and in health . . . until death do us part . . . unless I have to drop twenty dollars and then I'm outta here!"

Playing House

Vanessa met Jean Marc and they had a whirlwind courtship. Three months later, he professed his love, bought her a ring, and they decided to live together. She sold her condo, quit her job, and moved into his place an hour away. Soon after, she started noticing a change. Whereas before, he was respectful, he slowly became condescending toward her. Nine months later, she moved back out. Trivia question: What's wrong with this picture? Everything.

First is the timing issue. You never want to move in with a man after a few months or relocate to his stomping grounds. That's just way too soon. Also, when you move into his place, his "bachelor pad" is rarely going to be conducive for two. Because of this, it is highly unlikely that you will ever really feel like it's your place too. It will feel like a slumber party gone horribly wrong. If you try to change his place around to make it more suitable, he'll start feeling like he's giving up too much of his space. And you'll have to part with a lot of the stuff that makes you feel comfortable in your own home. All in all, not a good situation.

RELATIONSHIP PRINCIPLE 61

When you move into someone else's place,

you don't just give up

your personal space and belongings.

More important, nearly always you also lose

your *feeling of independence.*

When you bring two cats home together as kittens, they get along well. But if you bring a cat into another cat's territory, the cat whose territory it is will dominate the other little cat from then on. This is why women feel off balance when they move to a man's turf. It's a territorial thing.

Therefore, either let him move into your place (if there's enough room) or, better yet, go look for a place that is new to both of you. That is the best-case scenario because you'll be able to negotiate for everything you need. A closet of your own . . . a bathroom of your own . . . and anything else that floats your boat. And I highly recommend a king-size bed. Not for you. For him. It's the considerate, loving thing to do. It will prevent you from accidentally strangling him in your sleep because he hogs the bed and leaves you just enough room to dangle off the lower left corner of the queen mattress. Trust me: king size.

Let's assume he does have an enormous house, with a California king bed, and you move in. And let's say he's a multimillionaire with stupid money, and you end up quitting your job. At some point you still run the risk of having an argument, only to have him turn and say, "Where do you think you would be if you didn't have me? Look around. I provide you with *all of this*." This is precisely what you want to avoid. So the best thing to do is move into a new place *you both choose* together. Then, maintain your independence. Keep your job. Keep your friends. And definitely keep your own bank account and your own credit cards. It will give you the leverage to be treated how you want to be treated: with equality and justice for all.

Also, one quick final note:

RELATIONSHIP PRINCIPLE 62

If marriage is extremely important to you and you are ready to set a wedding date, don't move in unless you have a ring and a date.

If he's already "playing house," he won't have a reason to accelerate the process or take that next step.

Shotgun Weddings

This chapter would not be complete without one final discussion about pregnancy as it relates to marriage. It happens all the time and no one likes to talk about it. Yes, we are going to "go there."

Malena was dating a successful oncologist for six months. During that time, he was very good to her, but he made it very clear he didn't want children right away. Six months went by, and he hadn't proposed. Malena became increasingly impatient and "accidentally" got pregnant. Later, she admitted that she went off the Pill because they made her queasy (neglecting to mention that until it was too late). He tried everything to persuade her to terminate the pregnancy. In the end, she had her daughter and he turned out to be a great father. Just one glitch: He wanted nothing more to do with her. And Malena was stunned. She thought he'd have a chauffeur driving her around to go shopping all day (with the baby in its own separate limo).

Having a baby is one of life's biggest responsibilities, and you should never knowingly have a baby with someone if he *makes it a point to tell you* he doesn't want to be a father. You simply can't have a relationship based on mutual consideration and at the same time nullify a guy's right to make such an important choice. The reason it backfires speaks to the "attitude of entitlement" that men repeatedly said was a deal killer—whether it's a nice dinner, living together, or marriage and kids. After

Malena dropped her bombshell, to him she became the most unattractive woman in the world.

The father of the baby explained why it ruined her chances for marriage. "It's wonderful to have sex, right? But what if a man was to force you against your will? It would not be so wonderful anymore. That's how a guy feels about an unwanted pregnancy that he suspects is deliberate. If she shanghais the guy into it, he may love the child. But he will feel nothing but resentment toward the woman every time he looks at her. At that point she becomes frightening. What it tells him is that there is something very dangerous about her and that she is capable of anything. That's the woman who will sleep with your best friend and think nothing of it. Once a woman crosses a certain line, the odds of him marrying her, or even continuing to see her, are slim to none."

Men ultimately respect a bitch. Why? She's not a bitch because she's having a bad day. She's a bitch because she's a principled person who lives by her values. Standing up for yourself is one part of the equation. Being a stand-up person is the other part.

I've also heard several men tell stories about being engaged. And sometimes, during a heated blowup, some men ask for the ring back. In one instance, the guy's fiancée said no and claimed she had lost the ring (coincidentally that day). The next day, a mutual friend confided in him that she had pawned it. After that, the relationship was on again . . . off again.

She still wanted to get married, and for six months they had "break-up sex." But he refused to make a commitment because he couldn't get past feeling duped about the ring. Here's how most men think: If you appear honorable and say, "Here, I want you to have this ring back," he will say, "No, you keep it." His pride won't let him take it. But if you have a sense of entitlement or make him feel taken advantage of, he will want the ring.

If a man has any kind of substance and isn't as deep as a puddle, he'll have a couple of morals. What earns his respect is *decency*. Whenever I spoke with men about what they were looking for in a wife, I never once heard, "She has to be a good cook," or, "She has to wear Victoria's Secret lingerie every night." Instead what I heard time and time again was, "I want someone I can trust and count on."

RELATIONSHIP PRINCIPLE 63

The biggest turn-on for a man is knowing that he is in love with a woman he can really count on, who will *really* be there for him.

6

BREAKING INTO THE *Boys Club*

Stolen Secrets—All the Highly Classified Things Men Will Share Only in the Company of Other Men

A good marriage depends on the husband's ability to take a step back, and see where his wife *is wrong.*

~ARCHIE BUNKER

Highly Classified Secrets from My Covert Operatives

Brace yourself. This chapter will give you a rare glimpse inside the minds of some of the men I interviewed. As you'll witness, my information-gathering techniques would stump even Dirty Harry. Much of my scientific training was acquired in a very controlled setting. It began with a diet soda, a large bowl of popcorn, and watching back-to-back episodes of *Wildlife Journal* on Animal Planet.

In this chapter, you will hear the chattering of the male species from deep within the trenches of the dating jungle. To record the primates speaking, I did what any zoologist would do: I approached the creatures in a very nonthreatening way. I also learned not to approach during feeding time, for fear that they would growl and retreat back into their habitats for the winter.

I am also happy to report that my interrogations did not require any torture methods like the use of bright lights, sleep deprivation, electric prods, or playing reruns of *Little House on the Prairie*. Nor were they forced to watch *Ghost* with looped scenes of Demi Moore whimpering over her clay pot. I used no coercive methods whatsoever. At no time did I resort to the most horrifying threat of all: removal of one battery from the remote control.

We, here, at the headquarters of Bitches-R-Us, do not believe in animal testing. Therefore, no men were harmed *physically*. (I cannot comment on their current mental state.)

I now present to you my first subject. His name is Timmy. He is nine years old.

Sherry: How old are you, Timmy?

Timmy: I am nine years old.

Sherry: Can I interview you? I am writing a book.

Timmy: I am going to write a book too.

Sherry: What's the title?

Timmy: *Why Girls Are Dumb.*

Sherry: I hear you have a girlfriend. Is that true?

Timmy: Yes, her name is Sandy. And I know she has a crush on me.

Sherry: How do you know?

Timmy: Because she's really nice to all the boys . . . but *she's really mean to me.*

Timmy was the youngest of my interviewees. As men get older, they get more guarded about what they are willing to divulge to their partners. They feel that if they show their hand all the time, they'll lose control over their relationships. After all, certain sensitive subjects don't exactly make for good dinner conversation.

Most men were very open, but others were less comfortable revealing their secrets. I found that the guys who were "commitment material" were far more willing to talk about the types of tricks many of their friends use on women. I came to realize it's a little bit like breaking the law. (When you are doing something illegal, you don't want to go telling everyone about it.) That confirmed what I already knew: Men have a secret code with respect to commitment, marriage, and the inner workings of relationships.

I've excerpted some of the most truthful confessions in this chapter, verbatim. Here is what my "covert operatives" revealed. The men were from all walks of life, all nationalities, and all ages. Some were married, others were single. And with the exception of nine-year-old Timmy, I've withheld their names and identities (to protect the not-so-innocent).

Question 1: Do men mislead women about wanting commitment and marriage to get certain sexual "benefits"?

1. "Absolutely. A THOUSAND PERCENT."
2. "All guys know that their girlfriend will be

more sexually responsive and more emotionally understanding if she is made to believe their relationship has 'long-term potential.' All you have to do is use the right buzzwords, like *we* or *our* or *future* or *probably someday*. Men routinely use this to their advantage. 'I bet I could get her to do X, if I told her I was thinking of marrying her. *Someday*.'"

3. "If a man is seeing a woman, she'll usually let you know what she wants to hear. She projects to him what she needs to be told, and he says it. She makes the bed and he lies in it. It isn't until a year later she will start to get frustrated because she's not seeing any progress. He won't move in with you, he won't give you a key to his place, he won't even leave you alone in his place, and she doesn't have a ring. That's when she starts seeing that the relationship has reached its ceiling."

4. "Women think they are being sneaky, but if she's trying to drag me to a wedding every other Saturday, it's hardly subtle. If she starts putting pictures of the two of you everywhere, that is obvious as well. Let him be the one to put the picture up, otherwise he'll see it as the old fire-hydrant marking."

5. "Guys are tricky. If they have a big house in a nice area, they'll often use it as a hook. He may ask you to help pick out the paint for the 'baby room.' For when you have a kid together *someday*. And if periwinkle blue doesn't work out, it can always be one hell of a game room. Or he'll ask you to help him pick out furniture. If you tell a woman that you just bought a house and you

need help decorating it, she'll practically handcuff herself to you. And your bedpost."

6. "Men have relationships with women out of state. And women always think it's going to lead to something more. It won't. The guy gets off the plane, has sex all weekend, and then goes home. You can justify the come-and-go because you live in a different city. There's a built in excuse. Guys refer to this as a *long distance booty call*."

7. "Guys are sneaky. We have one friend who told his girlfriend, 'The only way I would get married is if a woman woke me up with a BJ every single morning.' The poor girl wore herself out every morning for three years, and he never proposed."

8. "What a man will do is tell the woman she's intelligent, funny, sophisticated, and that he's interested in her mind, and her soul (as he pulls her thong down). Essentially the goal is to make her feel like you don't see her as a sexual object. Then she thinks, 'Finally, a man who sees me as more than an object!' and she jumps in the sack with you. Men do it all the time. The goal is for her not to know what you are really after."

9. "Men act like the perfect lover boy. You'll say something like, 'I've never cheated on anyone. I'm not a kid anymore. My days of running with the boys are over, and I'm looking for something *real*. I'm more settled now and I have my eye out for Mrs. Right. I feel different with you. I feel like I could confide in you things that I

couldn't confide in anyone else.' When a guy comes on that strong, be careful. Usually the opposite is true. And if that's well delivered, he has most likely said it many times before."

10. "Some guys will call a lot, or seem very interested in boring conversation. I've actually fallen asleep during phone calls and woke up and said, 'Really? Then what happened?' And when a guy isn't really listening, that's a sign he's not interested in you. He's just biding his time until he gets into your pants."

There are two things to glean. First, if the wrong guy has too good a read on what you want (marriage, commitment, or material things), he'll use it to manipulate you. Pay close attention to the guy who said, "It's like giving a guy a manual on how to manipulate you. All he has to do is tell you what you want to hear, and it will take you a couple of years to figure it out."

A married man named Gene explained, "When a woman says, 'If you want to date me, you have to propose by the end of the year,' it goes over about as well as someone saying, 'I just wanted to go out tonight because I didn't feel like being at home.' In other words, the only thing he edged out was a rerun of *Seinfeld*. Instantly, you back off when you *aren't the reason* they are there."

RELATIONSHIP PRINCIPLE 64

Set your own timelines and limits, and leave if it's time to get out. Until then, don't let him know about your timelines or deal breakers. Then keep your eyes open and watch how he manages his 50 percent of the relationship. Then you'll get the real deal much quicker.

Question 2: How would you describe the traits of a confident woman (aka bitch) versus an insecure woman?

1. "The worst thing a woman can do is see a guy every night of the week. That's how she becomes his good-time girl on his 'reserve list.' What will happen is, the guy will start coming over at nine o'clock and then he'll leave by ten thirty. If he gets access or what he wants from her anytime he wants it, he won't have to lift a finger to keep it going."

2. "Men are competitive. When he buys a car that is a limited-edition model, he feels like he has something special. Guys in the street who race cars usually race for pink slips because they want to win, conquer, and take the other vehicle. That carries over to women. A woman who is easy won't scratch his competitive itch. When she stops expressing her opinion and starts agreeing with

everything he says, that's usually when a man starts to feel bored."

3. "A woman should never go looking for him or chase him down at three different places where he said he *might* be having a drink. If he says, 'Either I'll be at the Cheesecake Factory or some bar on Twenty-sixth,' don't try to track him down. If you want to be his 'steady,' let him come track you down."

4. "My fiancée was the first woman to put me in my place. She constantly reminds me, 'Hey, nobody's forcing you to stay.' If I try to BS my way out of a situation, she'd say, 'Let me save you the time and energy. Don't give me that shit, because I ain't buying it.' I know if she caught me cheating she'd smack me over the head with a frying pan. And I respect her more than any woman I've ever known."

5. "If he can sum you up in one sentence, he'll be bored."

6. "Confidence is when you don't try to interpret or overly process everything that you are observing out loud. It prevents the relationship from progressing on a normal course. For example, every time I gave this woman flowers, she would remind me that her ex stopped bringing her flowers. What she really wanted to ask was whether I'd keep doing it in the future. That made me feel like she didn't really enjoy the flowers, or appreciate the present moment with me."

7. "A woman shouldn't say, 'You don't call me enough,' or, 'You never tell me you love me.' As a

woman, your best asset is to be unpredictable. He should never be able to figure you out. When he can always predict what you are going to do next, you've lost him as a long-term partner. *He'll look for someone else, whom he can't understand or control."*

8. "If she feels strongly about something, she'll have a backbone. This woman is the woman he respects. Not a 'melba toast' cracker that crumbles with very little pressure."

9. "You have to seem like you aren't giving yourself fully. 'Here I am. Take me.' Men want to be kept guessing. Think about it. When a guy picks out a movie, he wants to be on the edge of his seat from the very beginning. If someone doesn't lose a limb or get shot and buildings aren't blown up all within the first twenty minutes, he'll think he got cheated out of twenty bucks."

10. "A woman shouldn't even crack a joke about marriage. I was on a second date with a girl and we are both from Ireland. Back home we have a saying, 'If you kiss me you are going to have to marry me.' If you have the desire to get married, never let a man know that up front. If you do, it's the same as handing him a manual and telling him exactly how to dangle a carrot and play on your weaknesses."

Question 3: What are the signs that a woman is wasting her time?

1. "When you get the nagging feeling you are always left hanging. If he's closing doors, saying things like 'gotta go' or 'talk to you later,' that means, 'I'll call you when it's your turn.' And don't listen to the 'I missed you so much' nonsense he tells you when he's coming around for sex. He won't disappear for a week at a time with a woman he's committed to."

2. "If he sees you one hour a week, it's casual. If you aren't going to the movies, meeting his friends, eating dinner together, and he says, 'I'm really not much of a phone guy' when he doesn't call—it is clear. With a woman he cares about, there will be consistent contact. A man will rarely break dates with a woman he's in love with."

3. "What a lot of guys do is say he's too busy working. Work never gets in the way of who he really wants to be with in his personal life. If a man really wants to see a woman, free time will magically appear."

4. "If a man is truly busy, he'll be specific about when he'll call you back. 'I'm tied up right now, but I will call you back X.' Then he specifies a date and time. But if he says, 'I'll get back to you,' and doesn't say when, that is a sign of disrespect. If he was out of town, same rule applies. If he can't reach you he'll pinpoint a day he'll be inaccessible—not a whole week."

5. "When you start hearing that the cell battery went dead, or the cell reception wasn't good, or he left his cell

phone in his car or at the office, he's not being honest with you."

6. "If it's been over two years and he won't give you a key to his apartment, you haven't met anyone from his family, and he won't discuss living together or marriage, it's not progressing because he doesn't want it to."

7. "A lot of guys keep women on a 'reserve list.' If he knows you'll always be there, he'll think, 'I know that one wants me, so let me put her on the reserve list and see who else is out there.' This is why you can never be too available, or let the guy get *too comfortable*. He has to worry that you won't be there."

8. "If a man says, 'Let's just keep things the way they are,' he's pretty much telling you that he doesn't see marriage on the horizon."

9. "When the relationship is based on comfort and familiarity. From the very beginning, there will be no effort. You can tell from the little things a man does or how he acts when he's around her. Does he walk her to her car? Will he drive out of his way? Or does he pull up to the curb and beep? And don't drive to his place in the late evening. It's a fool's errand."

10. "What a lot of guys will do is the 'jewelry store drive-by' with ring promised but not purchased. Or they'll look at a bridal magazine and say, 'You'd make a much prettier bride than her.' Then he has to get a promotion or a raise before he can afford to go through with it."

RELATIONSHIP PRINCIPLE 65

A guy who really thinks you could be "the one" will say very little about marriage. He'll be much more reserved, and will slowly open up over the course of several months, because he won't want to scare you off.

If he says things like, "Marriage is so antiquated. It's just a piece of paper. It's not really necessary. I have friends who have kids and have never gotten married. Who needs marriage?" keep him as a friend to go see a movie with, and don't close off your options.

Question 4: What secrets do men keep with regard to sex?

1. "Don't believe everything a guy tells you, especially in bed. One guy I know told a girl while they were having sex, 'I've always wondered what married sex feels like. Oh, baby. This is what it feels like to make love to my future wife. You are my dream. You are my shadow. Look at what you do to me.' It was the most sickening thing I've ever heard. No guy tells a woman he loves her and wants to marry her for the first time during sex. If a woman hears, 'I think I love you,' for the first time during a bump-and-grind session, she

should end the sex right there. That's a total con artist she's in bed with."

2. "The reason men watch shows like *Sex and the City* and *Desperate Housewives* is to learn about women. They worry, 'Is that what my girlfriend is really like?' It scares men that women are so fixated on these shows. We want to believe she's too innocent to be fascinated by anything that decadent."

3. "Never discuss your past, or your lack of a sexual past. A man doesn't want to think about another man on top of you working up a sweat. Whenever someone is trying to convince you they are a 'good girl,' there's a 90 percent chance that the opposite is true, so anything you say will make you look guilty. He'll think you knocked boots with the whole football team in high school and they retired *your* jersey when you graduated."

4. "If a woman gives a fantastic blow job the first time you are together, and she does it without hardly batting an eyelash, he'll be thinking, 'Where the hell did she learn how to do this?' If you seem like a pro, you might be a 'ho.'"

5. "If you sleep with him right away, he probably won't be around very long. With a one-night stand, deep down you *aren't doing something you are proud of.* You know that's not how it's supposed to be."

6. "Men don't tell women that half the things they see in porn are a bit silly and over the top. If the woman is screaming, 'Give it to me, Daddy' in bed, immediately I'll be concerned that she has a troubled past."

7. "A lot of women think pillow talk consists of confessions wrapped up in self-pity. After sex, you don't want to hear about what a woman doesn't like about herself or have to be the one to make her feel confident. I had one girl say, 'I wish my legs were longer from my knees to my ankles. And I hate my hips because they are so wide.' It tells the guy she has low self-worth and that she's easily taken advantage of."

8. "Sometimes a guy will call late and try to have sex with a woman. It may piss him off because she didn't say, 'Sure, come on over.' But the next day he feels more interested in her because she's not a fool. She keeps him honest and doesn't roll over and acquiesce to every whim."

9. "When a guy is in bed with a woman, if he's really turned on and he doesn't want to climax, he'll start thinking of things like sports, being in a locker room with a bunch of sweaty guys after a rugby game, yard work, and that leaky sink downstairs . . . anything to take his mind off the moment. He does not want to earn the title of 'five-minute man.'"

10. "I don't understand the appeal of the little-girl outfits. If a woman wears her hair in little braids at age thirty-five, and she has a little dog named Binky dressed in a pink sweater and matching jacket and a rhinestone leash, that's not going to get me in the mood. If a guy is into nasty little-girl stuff, he shouldn't be left alone with children unless he's closely supervised."

A lot of the men admitted that although the "instant gratification" part of them wants to have sex on the first date, if they really want to have a lasting relationship, they prefer to wait. He really wants that diamond of a woman, someone whom he can really be proud of. If he ends up in the sack with you on the first date, he won't see you as "the one." Moreover, when he tells you all the things *he thinks* you want to hear, and you seem unimpressed or nonchalant, he'll usually start to pursue you on a more honest level.

Question 5: Why do men test women? And is it done purposefully?

1. "Yes, it's conscious. The reason men test women is we believe that if you are going to be spending your life with someone, you really have to see who she is from all sides. You want to know if she's crazier than a road lizard, or whether she'll be compatible with you."

2. "Most men see women as too emotional. This is why he'll give you a rundown of all his ex-girlfriends. While some escape with just being called a drama queen, others are labeled psychos (otherwise known as schizos). Every guy talks about that one psycho ex, with that one episode in which she lost it, and the men in white coats had to come and throw a net over her, and shoot her with a tranquilizer dart. You know, just like they do with a dangerous animal that escaped from the zoo."

3. "What a guy will do is watch a woman when another woman walks in the room. If she's the least bit jealous it will show all over her face. Then all he has to do is say that that woman has on a pretty dress, or she has nice hair, or she has a nice walk. And he knows that is all it takes to set off his girlfriend. She'll get so pissed, steam will be coming off of her. The truth is, he doesn't really give a damn about the other woman, he just wants to rile up his girlfriend. It may sound immature, but we want to know you still care."

4. "Let's say you've made a statement that you don't like it when someone is late. That gets stored in his memory bank. If he wants to test you, he'll show up an hour late with a good story. If you scream, shout, or curse, he won't think of you as marriage material. A calm reaction is, 'I was a little worried about you, but I'm glad you are here. Give me a call next time.' That tells you she is classy and graceful and, most important, she can be reasoned with. And that's the woman you'll consider marrying."

5. "Don't ask, 'Do I look fat in these jeans?' A guy might answer, 'Not too fat. Just stop eating all that ice cream.' What he's doing is keeping you insecure so that you'll work harder to please him. A lot of men think that giving lukewarm compliments to a woman makes it easier for them to manipulate her. If you need to be complimented constantly, men will assume you aren't secure with yourself."

6. "Part of a guy feeling comfortable with a woman has to do with how she treats him after he screws up. It's a little like dealing with your mother. Every man knows when he's doing something wrong. If I do something out of line, and my wife doesn't go to the gutter to address it, it wins my respect. That's a big turn-on to a guy."

7. "When a guy is in love, he won't go out drinking or fishing as much. But he still wants to do it every once in a while. If he wants to go to a strip bar, he understands that it's disrespectful. But if he wants to go to a football game, be supportive. Ask if you can get any hot dogs for the tailgating party. This way he'll be thinking that marriage to you will be a lot of fun, and that he won't be missing out on the other little things he enjoys."

8. "A woman cannot go off and have emotional outbursts all the time. He'll slowly lose respect for her, especially if she does it in front of his children. The most unattractive thing a woman can do is stomp her feet like a child. You don't ever want him to think of you like that."

9. "It's extremely important for a man to maintain his love and lust for a woman. If there's always drama, his sexual attraction will slowly turn off like a dimmer switch. Every time she is reasonable, strong, and rational—it makes a man want to give her the world."

10. "You have to be willing (or at least pretend to be willing) to listen to what he has to say. When a man

feels he's really being listened to, or understood, that gives him hope that you can have a positive outcome. He has to think you don't rush to judgment, and that you'll listen. Even when he's telling you a bunch of BS, you can still listen. That gives you more credibility when you say, 'No chance in hell I'm ever going to buy that crap. If this ever happens again, I suggest you come up with a better excuse than that because that BS is not going to fly.'"

Now that you've heard it directly from the horse's mouth, remember not to get your panties in a ruffle. He's not doing it to get a perverse thrill, but rather to get attention. It's like a toddler in a high chair who throws his rattle down on the floor. Why? So Mommy will come pick it up. Then Mommy comes and picks it up and gives the rattle back to the toddler. And what does the toddler do? He throws it down again. Why? To get attention.

RELATIONSHIP PRINCIPLE 66

The more control you have over yourself, the more of a hold you will have on his heart.

A person with self-control is a person who can get up and leave at any time. Men instinctively know this, which is why self-control raises the benchmark of how he treats you. Adopt the attitude, "I refuse to walk around like an exposed raw nerve. I've made up my mind that I'm going to be upbeat, positive, and I won't believe what other people tell me about myself." This is true empowerment and confidence. And it not only makes you a man magnet, it will make you a people magnet as well.

Question 6: What are men secretly afraid of?

1. "Men are afraid of being stuck with the wrong woman, particularly someone who makes him miserable. He's afraid she'll nag him like his mom did, and start looking like his grandmother did. He's not afraid of a wrinkle or two. He's afraid she'll transform into someone he doesn't recognize, who he couldn't imagine going to bed with."

2. "Men are afraid of having to compete with your BOB (**B**attery **O**perated **B**oyfriend). He wants to believe his magic pole is doing the job, and if you use BOB in front of him and it gets the job done quicker and better, he's going to lose his desire because he knows he can't compete with that."

3. "Men are afraid of showing weakness. If I've had a really crappy day, I may not want to talk about 'feelings' with my partner. I might even avoid seeing her altogether because I don't want to take it out on her.

As a man, you want to be strong for a woman you care about."

4. "He's afraid of a woman driving his car. Men feel that most women don't appreciate equipment and fine craftsmanship. A man's car is his pride and joy. It never fails. A woman will open a door onto a curb and crash it right into a newsstand. But if he really loves a woman, he'll let her drive the car. Once or twice. It's a symbolic gesture. That means he trusts her and values her more than the car."

5. "Men are afraid of losing status or of falling apart emotionally, and not being able to pull himself together. That's why men meet at the campfire to cowboy up. Once you have a couple of beers with the guys, your problems tend to go away. That's why men don't want to see themselves lying on some shrink's couch, with someone handing him a tissue."

6. "A guy's biggest fear is that his wife will cheat on him. Most men are very afraid of that happening, especially after there are children involved. Men have thoughts that run through their minds. He knows if it ever happened, he would be faced with having to weigh the emotional welfare of his children versus his own emotional welfare. It's the kind of thing that ruins lives."

7. "I'm deadly afraid of having stupid kids. That's why I couldn't marry a woman who had a blank stare. No guy wants a glassed-over look, or a lifeless woman with no spark. You know the type—the ones where you

begin to wonder if there was too much inbreeding with the cousins."

8. "Men want to have a good-looking wife, but they are afraid of being held to the same standard. Men wouldn't be able to handle it if he was crazy about a woman and was put under the same scrutiny. If his wife said, 'Hey, you are starting to have a potbelly, and I'm not feeling so attracted to you.' That would make him feel the heat, and he'd head straight to the gym."

9. "Men are afraid to be made into suckers, fools, or to be taken advantage of. No guy wants to be suckered into becoming a meal ticket. If you are a meal ticket, you feel cheap. Then you have resentment that begins to grow, and you start to feel that all women can't be trusted."

10. "Men fear divorce, because it's a woman's world in the divorce court. And if you have kids, your goose is cooked."

The pressure to be "manly" will influence how he approaches a relationship. Remember, men don't have different feelings from women, just a different style. It doesn't matter how unemotional they seem, men are vulnerable as well. They, too, can get squashed like a grape. A man has a deep need to be validated, and he often won't tell you when he feels vulnerable. If he's bothered he'll say, "Aw, hey, that's no problem," even though he could be crying on the inside.

RELATIONSHIP PRINCIPLE 67

If a man really cares, he feels vulnerable. That's when he needs a protective shield the most and that's when he'll often behave more coolly.

Question 7: What is the best way for a woman to reignite a man's interest if it might be starting to cool off?

1. "She shouldn't."

2. "If a guy isn't keeping up the routine of what he's doing, she should stop all the calls. Make him think you lost interest, and become scarce. She should become unavailable and stop sleeping with him. He needs to think, 'Wait a minute? She usually calls by now.'"

3. "It's the old saying, 'You don't miss the water till the well runs dry' Cut off the water supply with no explanation and no reason. The best thing a woman can do is cut off contact with no explanation and let him come through with a grand gesture."

4. "If a guy staggers in at 3:00 A.M., don't be home when he gets home. Call up a girlfriend and stay over at her place. That will be an instant wake-up call."

5. "One guy I know would stop off to have a drink every day after work. Then he'd wait for his girlfriend to start calling him and beg, 'Come home. When are

you coming home?' One time she didn't call. He started calling the house and the phone just rang. Then he got up and ran home looking for her. Suddenly, going home became interesting. But as long as she was waiting on him, he was bored."

6. "One girl I dated would say to me, 'I'll call you right back, in five minutes. I'm right in the middle of something.' Then I wouldn't hear from her. That's when I realized I was taking her for granted and redoubled my efforts."

7. "To rekindle his interest, split for the weekend with the girls. Tell him you are going on a trip and don't call while you're gone."

8. "She can call him out. She can say, 'Listen, if I'm taking up your time here, and you are feeling like you'd rather be somewhere else, that's cool. There's someone out there for everyone.' If she recognized it and called him on it, it lets him know that she's in tune to what's going on and she isn't too accepting of disrespect. That keeps him on his toes."

9. "Pick up your own hobby. Don't wait on him. Get busy with something else so he is unsure when he can see you."

10. "You never want to be like a dog that waits at the door. An animal will wait for you because it makes its day. If you become like that, you'll become disinteresting. But if you always explore new things, and he can see you are growing independently, he will respect you. There's nothing more attractive than a woman who is

passionate about her own life and discovers new things. He'll work to be a part of that, and he'll work to keep himself just as interesting."

RELATIONSHIP PRINCIPLE 68

Whenever boredom sets in, simply break the routine. As soon as the routine changes, it will pique his interest and the relationship will become interesting again.

Question 8: How can a woman tell if a man's really in love and thinking about forever?

1. "He's dunking for two, not one. He'll create things to do, and he'll be thinking for two—rather than thinking for one. He'll start making important life choices with you in mind. Where he lives, what house he buys, the trips he takes. The bachelor outings will become a once-in-a-while thing to see his friends for an occasional pool game. You'll become his favorite best friend to spend time with. If he has one week of vacation, he's planning it with you, not his long-lost buddy from college."

2. "His interest will be consistent. If he's thinking long-term, there won't be severed contact. He won't

give his time sporadically and he won't contact you every now and then. On the other hand, when everything else in the world comes before you and you start hearing, 'My second cousin's brother's father-in-law's sister needs me to watch the kids, so I can't see you all weekend,' it's not about love. When he truly cares, you won't get the on-again, off-again intermittent contact. You'll have continuous access and you'll know all aspects of his life."

3. "He'll be on his toes a little with her. When a guy cares about you, he's much more alert and wants to please you. He has a certain sweat and a nervousness about him. You can call him any time of the day and ask him for something. If you walk up on a puddle of water, you get the feeling that he would throw his jacket over it. You aren't just taking up physical space like a piece of furniture. You occupy his mind and his thoughts also, and he feels a little tingle when he's with you."

4. "He won't give excuses. There will be no degrees and levels to love. No 'I love you but I'm not *in* love with you.' When a man is in love, he may have a bad day every now and then, but he doesn't waffle about wanting to be with you. If someone is separating love into different categories, making distinctions between love with a cherry on top and love with only whipped cream, then that's not love."

5. "If he really enjoys talking to you at the end of the day, that's a huge sign. When a man is in love with you, he'll call almost every day throughout the week,

not just on weekends. When you drive somewhere or go to dinner, you never run out of things to talk about."

6. "He won't ask you out by always saying, 'Feel free to stop by.' He'll want to see you on an appointment basis because it's special. He'll be thinking, 'Let me build up to this. Let me drag this out.' That's when you know you are a prize—not just a piece."

7. "He'll be in your corner, even when you are wrong. His friends won't be able to put you down, and he'll be protective of your feelings. If a female co-worker calls him at midnight, he will ask her not to call that late. You will always feel like you are number one in his life."

8. "He will give you open access to his life. You won't get less attention after six months than he gave in the first month. At a certain point, he'll even let you answer his phone. Almost anything he does, you'll be invited to do with him."

9. "He'll go out of his way. With a woman he's crazy about, he'll put in all the overtime in the world. He'll be doing things for you, he'll be considerate, he'll want to please you, he'll try to cheer you up if you are down, and he will enjoy every moment because you are the person he values most."

10. "He'll ask you to marry him."

Above all, *he will respect you as a woman*. When a man is in love with you, he'll never refer to you as a "chick" or a "girl" or "his old lady" or his "ball and chain." He'll refer to you as his woman, or his girlfriend, or his wife, or his fiancé. He'll refer to you *with respect*, because he sees you as the girl of his dreams.

7

FROM "I MIGHT" TO "I Do"

Getting a Ring on the Finger That He's Wrapped Around

Protect yourself so that nobody overrides you, overrules you, or steps on you. Just say, "Just a minute. I'm worth everything, dear."

~MAYA ANGELOU

Stepping off the Marry-Go-Round

In a perfect world, Romeo meets Juliet. After a year of a whirlwind courtship, he rents a Lear jet, flies her to a private island, and drops to one knee and proposes. Then fireworks light up the sky, the planets align, birds are chirping, dogs and cats go skipping into the sunset, and everybody goes home happy.

Reality check: More often than not, proposals don't happen like they do in the movies. You may get a good ring, or a good proposal, but they don't always come together (unless he's got a great scriptwriter, or has spent a lot of time in the Hallmark aisle). Sometimes there's no fanfare at all. Behind closed doors the guy is saying, "All right, all right. We'll go look at rings, I promise. There's two minutes left in the Super Bowl. Can we discuss this another time?"

Ever notice that men act funny when a jewelry commercial comes on? The reason men hate these ads is that they can literally feel the tension thicken in the room. *"For Valentine's Day, show her that you love her. Diamonds are forever."* Then they show a woman beaming with joy, with sappy music in the background. Then the bride and groom running down the beach in their gown and tux. *"May your love last as long as the diamond does."* After the commercial is over, his girlfriend is looking down at her left hand with a sad pouty face, like a little girl who dropped her ice cream cone. Like a cartoon, an imaginary bubble pops up over her head. "Where the hell is my ring?" Meanwhile, the bubble over his head reads, "Which Madison Avenue asshole decided to interrupt my playoffs with this crap?"

Since most women generally are at a loss to find the right language to talk about engagement, this chapter will help you improve your skills in that area. The information you are about to read is based on the feedback I gathered from a number of men who have either recently gotten engaged or are already married. The first thing all men unanimously agreed on was the following:

RELATIONSHIP PRINCIPLE 69

You have a much better chance of getting engaged when a man doesn't feel pressured into it.

When it comes to the "negotiations," the bitch's approach works better than the typical nice girl's attempts to get a proposal. The bitch doesn't pout. She doesn't hint. She doesn't nag. For a whole year, there is none of that. She goes out, has fun, and doesn't tip her hand or discuss commitment. Why? Because a year or so later, he is attached. He is powerfully hooked. He finds her desirable to be around. She doesn't represent pressure . . . or an obligation. She is a prize he worked for and won . . . almost. All of this gives her clout.

The bitch's approach is subtle, for two reasons. First, she understands that guys aren't stupid. He doesn't have to be the spelling-bee champ to understand that most women wouldn't exactly consider the relationship a smashing success if they simply lived with a guy for years on end. Unless he was raised by a pack of wolves, he knows this much.

The second reason she keeps her approach subtle is that if it's been a year, asking him "Where is this going?" is moot. If he hasn't brought it up, asked you to marry him, or given a serious indication that he's going to soon, it's crystal clear where it's *going*: He is trying to have his cake and eat it too.

A newlywed named Jeff explained:

"I'd lived with other women before I got married to my wife.

And all guys know that after a year or two at the most, the woman loses a bit of her dignity. *And truthfully, you lose respect for the woman if she stays, because on some level the guy knows the relationship has become a free ride. He knows he's getting all the perks without giving anything up. If the woman wants to get married and he's stalling for a couple of years, he knows he's taking advantage of the woman.*

Or he knows he can ride it out, until he's ready to leave. If she is willing to stick around, the guy is thinking, 'Oh good, I don't have to marry her.' But then you begin to think, 'Why is she letting me have a free ride?' There is something wrong with her."

In other words, he begins to lose respect. He assumes she is naïve . . . or desperate. She becomes less appealing because he knows he's taking advantage of her and she's not standing up for herself. As they say in Hollywood, "They'll kill you with encouragement."

This is often when the devaluing process begins. "Why do I need to prize and cherish her?" An even more basic assumption lies below this one: "I have the option to keep her until I get tired of her. Or until something better comes along. I'll enjoy this until I feel like going back to my bachelor life." And this is precisely the level of security a bitch will not allow a man to have.

RELATIONSHIP PRINCIPLE 70

The bitch won't allow herself to be with a man who is biding his time until something better comes along.

This directly relates to why men marry bitches. *A bitch has strength of conviction.* As painful as it is, as afraid as she might feel—she will leave if she doesn't get what she wants. And guess what? That's precisely why she gets what she wants. When a bitch *subtly* gets the point across that she *won't* wait forever, it becomes the same as any other negotiation. When one person is willing to walk off the showroom floor, the other person has to come up with a better offer.

That said, you can't give him an ultimatum. But here's what you can do: You can have one or two conversations with him. The first conversation is a fact-gathering session. And if you don't like what you hear, in the second conversation you lower the boom.

If it's been a year and you want him to propose, the first conversation should be one where you are very matter-of-fact. Say something like:

We've been going out for a year. I love you and think you are wonderful. And I accept things as they are. But I'd like a little bit more from a relationship than what we have right now and this doesn't really seem to be progressing.

(Then, be silent.)

The less you say after that, the more power you will have. The objective is to create a nonthreatening opening for him in a very casual way. Your job is to keep a poker face and show no emotion. Why? You want to get the truth. You don't want lip service or to be told what he thinks you want to hear—you want to get his *real* answer. He may tell you he's madly in love with you and he's been planning a surprise. Then he might hint about going away for the weekend. Or, he might ask if you want to shop for a ring.

If he doesn't give you the answer you want to hear, and you get a vibe that he's avoiding the subject at all costs, that's your cue to become scarce. Whatever time you normally spend with him, cut that back 60 to 70 percent. See him once or twice in a two-week period. Then plan a weekend getaway with the girls. (That always petrifies them because they don't know what your friends might tell you.) If he asks you whom you are seeing, assure him you aren't seeing anyone else. Just keep yourself busy and outside his reach. But don't explain why. *He will know.*

RELATIONSHIP PRINCIPLE 71

The bitch does not hint about marriage or ask, "Where is this going?" Instead, she hints about the removal of herself from the relationship.

The word* marriage *never even comes up.

Rest assured, he'll get it. Within a couple of weeks, it's likely that another conversation will come up because he will notice a change and ask you, "What's wrong?" When he does, you don't want to seem as though you are let down, devastated, or upset. If he is still not telling you he wants the relationship to move forward, you may want to consider telling him the following:

"We've had a wonderful time. And I don't regret the time we've spent together. I think the world of you. But obviously we want different things, so we need to do the right thing. I love you and I want you to be happy, I want you to have what you are looking for also. I think it's time for us to move on."

This is when you have to be classy and show him that you are different. No late-night drama. No crying. No guilt trips. No martyr or victim on the premises. Don't give him the impression that you feel you've been shortchanged. And don't have any further conversations with him. This is not a beg-a-thon.

The reason silence is golden at this point is that anything you say after that will let him know he can buy time, stall, or "okeydoke" you. Any weeping or crying in a discussion like this will show him you are unsure, and he'll think he doesn't have to change a thing. *What it tells him is you can be manipulated and he doesn't have to take you seriously.*

Simply emphasize what you want, and then appear strong and mature. "I don't want you getting into something that you are not ready for." If you are calm, it scares a man far more, because then he knows it's not a hormone-driven decision. You've based it on what he's offering, who he is, and what he has shown you he is willing to contribute. And you don't intend to settle because you don't see yourself as desperate. This raises your stock. "Uh-oh. I have to give her a reason to stay, or I will lose her."Now let's recap:

- He doesn't get an ultimatum.
- He doesn't get pressure, hear "marry me, marry me," or have the feeling he's being tied up like a Thanksgiving turkey.
- You are mature, open, honest, and nonjudgmental.
- You aren't shooting the relationship down, expressing anger that he's "milking the cow for free," or telling him he screwed up.
- You simply said, "You are fun, neat, and cool, and I love you. But before we waste any more of each other's time, we need to get this thing figured out."

It's not what you say, it's *how you hold yourself when you leave*. You have to hold yourself with a calm that is unlikely given the circumstances. Then he thinks, "Hmmm. This one is a cat of a different breed." Then you become irreplaceable. It's all about character, and it's all about class.

Men are socialized to believe that women are the weaker sex. So when you are willing to stand on your principles even though it might be painful or it might cost you something, you become the ultimate warrior. "Wait a minute. I had her. Now I can't get my way with her. What's going on here?" When you can pull back, collect yourself, and act like you are aware of what's going on, guess who comes out on top?

This is what most men are looking for in a wife. This is their ultimate dream girl—a feminine woman who is not ruled by emotions and insecurity. There's a quiet dignity about certain women. It's like a force field around her that melts him like butter. She doesn't scream. She doesn't shout. Her subdued self-worth and faith in herself is the true essence of what makes her a bitch.

Jessica and Rick are a perfect example of this dynamic. They were together for three years and had a great relationship. Nevertheless, he was dragging his feet with respect to marriage.

Jessica then said, "If you don't want to marry me after three years, we should go our separate ways. Bye-bye." I remember her telling me this story and waving her hand as she said "Bye-bye." Then she cut off all contact. Three months later, Rick called Jessica and asked, "Can I see you for dinner tomorrow night. Please?" She declined. He kept persisting every night. She finally agreed, reluctantly. At dinner, he proposed with a beauty of a ring.

It's how men think. If a quarterback gets sacked and leveled by a very hard hit, he'll get back up. It won't faze him, and he'll still try to throw his touchdowns.

If you are backing away and he asks, "Can we still see each other sometimes?" tell him, "Of course." Then, every time he wants to see you, be unavailable to see him. Take your time with him from 60 to 70 percent available down to a 97 percent unavailable. Avoid him *without* the appearance of doing so. This will allow his imagination to run wild. That's when the loneliness and the lack of companionship will begin to set in.

What you *don't* want to do is talk openly about seeing other men. Why? No need. He will already be petrified at the thought of another man penetrating his woman. "Another guy is going to deliver something I can't deliver?" Then he will start envisioning you being serenaded and serviced by some other man (who might do it better), which will be enough to drive him over the edge. He's been sleeping with you for a year, and in his mind you were built just for him. The thought of another man is . . . *unthinkable*. This is why you have to make yourself scarce, so that the *unthinkable* starts to be *thought* about over and over . . . to the degree that it keeps him up nights. That's when he'll make a beeline to the nearest jewelry shop.

Every man *thinks* he wants his freedom . . . that is, until he gets it. Then, separation anxiety coupled with meeting a woman in a bar who says, “What kind of car do you drive?” makes him realize he’s losing the best thing he’s ever had.

I call this my “beer nuts analogy.” If you are a good woman, you represent his relationship diet. You are a healthy breakfast, lunch, and dinner. Some other girl he might get attention from represents beer nuts. And as long he gets three meals a day at home, he can grab a little attention, or a few beer nuts, with a cold beer with the guys. But when you remove yourself from the equation altogether, he has to make three meals out of beer nuts. That’s when he quickly realizes the grass isn’t so green on the other side. “Hey, these are crappy beer nuts.”

Remember, you want to take the high road. Don’t subtly threaten him that you will be dating other men, because it goes without saying. He will feel like you are trying to hold something over his head: “Do what I say, or else.” To some men, this is terribly offensive. “If I don’t get what I want when I want it, I’ll throw everything we had away in a heartbeat.” That makes it seem like the relationship may not be worth “forever.”

Jane and Darren were dating and she gave him a direct ultimatum after one year. Two weeks later, he stopped by and was going to propose. And when he came in, she proceeded to show him all the e-mails she was getting from a guy she had already gone out with a few times. She did not know at the time that he had a ring in his pocket. Although he was devastated, he saw it as a sign that the relationship wasn't worthy of forever.

At the end of the day, your character and willingness to stand by your convictions are all he can really rely on. He knows that the wrong woman can ruin him emotionally and financially. When a bitch stands up for what she believes in a decent and honest way, it brings all his emotions to the surface. The relationship becomes very real. There is a genuineness and an authenticity about her. By being willing to tell him, "I'm putting it all on the line and I'm willing to walk out on comfort and security to get what it is I truly want," he'll often feel that he needs the woman. He can't exist without her. That's when she becomes "the one."

RELATIONSHIP PRINCIPLE 72

When you stand up for yourself in a dignified, feminine, and womanly way, you can get *anything* you want from a man. When you place a high value on yourself *in the right way*, so will he.

Sometimes it takes minutes for him to come around, other times it takes weeks or months. If he's in love with you he will come around. And if he doesn't, *he would have wasted your time for five years or ten years* and you would have ended up with the exact same outcome. *So you lost nothing.*

So give the guy a chance to propose. After all, men aren't predisposed or conditioned to think about marriage. He's not lying in bed at night dreaming of a gondola ride for two in Italy, with both of you being serenaded by a guy with a thick accent singing "O Solo Mio," to the strum of a little guitar. However, a year has gone by and now he's attached. And now you are not so easily replaced or forgotten.

Whereas women fall in love in a man's presence, men tend to realize they are in love in a woman's absence. And sometimes all he needs is a little time to make that realization.

Changing the Lens You See Yourself Through

In one of her diary entries, Marilyn Monroe wrote that when she was walking down the street with Joe DiMaggio, she felt like he should walk on the inside of the curb and she should "walk in the gutter." She was arguably the most beautiful woman in the world—a legend. And even with all her beauty and sex appeal, she had the nagging feeling that many nice girls share because of low self-worth—like an anchor is dragging them down in life.

When choosing a wife, men notice whether you are happy. Or, whether you feel good about yourself. Michelle and Michael are happily married, and when they were dating she said something to him that he remembered years later: "If I'm married, I'm going to be very happy. And if I'm single I'm going to live a great life and be happy also. So it's not really a priority." This is precisely what a bitch brings to a relationship that an insecure "nice girl" does not. A joy of life . . . a joie de vivre.

What is the difference between Michelle, an ordinary woman, and the legendary Marilyn Monroe? It boils down to this:

RELATIONSHIP PRINCIPLE 73

In life, half the battle has to do with the lens you choose to see yourself through. Your fulfillment hinges on whether you see yourself through a positive lens or a negative one.

If you don't feel like you are "enough" *without* a husband, you will not feel like you are "enough" with a husband. If you see yourself through a negative lens, you will tell yourself things like, "What's wrong with me?

All my friends are married . . . *except me.*" Being single doesn't make you less than . . . any more than marriage is a guarantee for happiness. If that were the case, half the marriages wouldn't end in divorce.

However, seeing yourself through a positive lens is the best chance at happiness you've got. Enjoy every day. Live it to the fullest. Be positive. Love yourself. And screw what anyone else thinks if they don't approve of you. Don't let anyone darken your doorstep. Otherwise, when you get married, you will still be unhappy and, like Marilyn Monroe, you will feel like you belong in the gutter.

As you have heard from men throughout this book, a man desires . . . craves . . . and holds out for a strong, spirited woman who knows who she is. He doesn't want to feel like he's adopting an orphan or taking in a needy child who apologizes for her need, can't speak her mind, and needs someone else to tell her if she's worthy. So don't think about "happy endings" . . . think about a happy beginning. And start that today . . . regardless of your marital status.

Why does this make you more likely to find a husband? A married man named Mark explained, "Men know that if a woman isn't happy with herself, if he marries her he will become the recipient of her disillusionment, and resentment. It will become 'all his fault' that she's not a happy person. This is why men are instinctively drawn to a woman who is happy with him . . . or without him."

It's why men marry bitches: A guy will be less likely to worry about losing his freedom to a woman who doesn't appear to need him to make her happy.

Of course, this is isn't what women are taught. In the movie *The Joy Luck Club*, there's a scene that typifies the self-abnegating, doting behavior that Rose uses to win her husband over, not understanding why it's having the opposite effect. "I told myself that was the loving way. Over time, I could see that Ted was becoming bored. *So I tried harder*." Then it cuts to a scene in which she and her husband have a discussion about what they'll be having for dinner (which is painful for him because she's become silent to everyone . . . including herself).

Rose: Honey, should we eat in, or go out to eat tonight?

Ted: You decide.

Rose: If we eat in I have lamb chops. Or I could call Square One. I didn't mean to interrupt your work.

Ted: You're not interrupting me. Really I meant what I said. I want to hear what *you* want.

Rose: You've had a hard day and I don't really care. I just want you to be happy . . . Honey, what's wrong?

Ted: It's just that once in a while I'd like to hear what you want. I'd like to hear *your* voice, even if we disagree. You used to be different. You used to have an opinion.

Notice how apologetic she is, or how afraid she is to impose. She sees herself as an imposition . . . as lower than him. That is her lens. Later, when she changes that lens, she gets a backbone and her husband's respect reignites.

In a magazine article, Meg Ryan said, "In my everyday life, I find myself apologizing for a need . . . or the way I feel about something. I don't want to live like that anymore." And I submit to you that you shouldn't either.

RELATIONSHIP PRINCIPLE 74

Men rarely take it as a compliment when you bend over backward or become too agreeable. Men want to feel special, and when you are *too nice* he feels ordinary, because he assumes you'd acquiesce and become a yes-person with *any man*.

Most "nice girls" are given the wrong information. They are taught the following:

- "If I show him I love him every few hours, it will sink in and he'll love me more."
- "If I 'go along to get along,' he'll think we are more compatible."

- "If I sacrifice myself, I will better our relationship."
- "If I always agree with him, he'll think more highly of my opinions."
- "If I look good, I'll get the respect I want."
- "If I double my efforts, it will double his appreciation."

Then she pleases him right out the door. A man will lose respect and be less likely (not more) to commit whenever he senses that:

- His decision is the final say.
- He is the authoritative figure in the relationship.
- He can do no wrong in your eyes.
- You assume an inferior place in the relationship.

You will never prove to a man that you are the best thing to happen to him by bowing down or compromising yourself. Nor will you prove you are more "worthy" by kissing a man's ass . . . because *then you won't have his respect.* Deep down, men don't find it emotionally fulfilling to be in a relationship that makes him feel as if he's being idolized by an underling.

RELATIONSHIP PRINCIPLE 75

He doesn't marry a woman who puts him on a throne. He marries a woman who is his equal . . . that special woman whom he can share all of life's special moments with.

A man wants to feel like he is your hero. Men need to feel validated. He wants to feel that you admire him, look up to him, and that he is the protective one in the relationship. *But he wants that from a self-respecting woman who has a backbone and who first and foremost loves herself.*

So begin with changing your lens . . . or sharpening your focus. Change the way you see yourself, be careful of those who try to convince you of who you are. If they can convince you that you are ugly when you are beautiful . . . that you are stupid when you are smart . . . that you are incapable when you are capable . . . they can also convince you that you are not worthy when you really are. So don't believe what anyone tells you about yourself. When you do, and their view of you is negative . . . you lose your feelings and your opinions. You become afraid to approach . . . afraid to be bold . . . afraid to pursue new heights. You become silent to everyone . . . including yourself. And that's how you lose the most precious commodity you have to bring to a marriage—you.

Before we end, I think it's important to do one last thing. Let's rewrite the fairy tale, shall we? Let's forget everything we learned in Cinderella, Sleeping Beauty, and Dorothy, Toto, and the Land of Oz—and let's give the fairy tale a little makeover. The storybook ending should read like this:

Once upon a time there was a princess. Along came a prince who asked her if she'd like to ride on his white horse. She said, "I'd like to take a ride on your horse, but I can't right now because I'm a little busy getting my own horse. Go ride off into the sunset without me, and I'll catch up to you a little later." Suddenly, the prince is dumbfounded. He's never heard anything like this before. Something clicks inside him, and it starts a fire within him that he can't put out, because she doesn't need him. And then he says, "I have to be with her for the rest of my life."

Then they fall in love, marry, and ride off into the sunset. And then she tortures him . . . *lovingly ever after.*

The End

SHERRY'S RELATIONSHIP *Principles*

RELATIONSHIP PRINCIPLE 1

In romance, there's nothing more attractive to a man than a woman who has dignity and pride in who she is.

RELATIONSHIP PRINCIPLE 2

He marries the woman who *won't* lay down like linoleum.

RELATIONSHIP PRINCIPLE 3

He doesn't marry a woman who is perfect. He marries the woman who is *interesting*.

RELATIONSHIP PRINCIPLE 4

When a woman is trying too hard, a man will usually test to see how hard she's willing to work for it. He'll start throwing relationship Frisbees, just to see how hard she'll run and how high she'll jump.

RELATIONSHIP PRINCIPLE 5

Don't believe what anyone tells you about yourself.

RELATIONSHIP PRINCIPLE 6

Men see how you dress, and then make assumptions about your relationship potential.

RELATIONSHIP PRINCIPLE 7

When a man sees you wearing very revealing clothes, he'll usually assume you don't have anything else going for you.

RELATIONSHIP PRINCIPLE 8

When he sees you scantily dressed, he is not reminded of how great you look naked. He immediately thinks of all the other men you've slept with.

RELATIONSHIP PRINCIPLE 9

Every guy knows he can find a girl who is simply satisfied with satisfying *him*. They are much more turned on by a woman who cares about her own pleasure as well.

RELATIONSHIP PRINCIPLE 10

You can tell how much someone respects you by how much he respects your opinion. If he doesn't respect your opinion, *he won't respect you*.

RELATIONSHIP PRINCIPLE 11

It is better to be disliked for being *who you are* than to be loved for *who you are not*.

RELATIONSHIP PRINCIPLE 12

Men like to be curious. They like to feel that there's more to the story than what they already know.

RELATIONSHIP PRINCIPLE 13

The mental challenge is not, "Can I get her to sleep with me?" The mental challenge is, "Can I get *and keep* her attention?"

RELATIONSHIP PRINCIPLE 14

Your power gets lost the minute you start asking, "Where do I stand?" Because what you've just told him is that the terms of the relationship are now *his to dictate.*

RELATIONSHIP PRINCIPLE 15

As soon as a man has his guard up, he will not fall in love or get attached. *The only way he'll get attached is if you lower his guard first.*

RELATIONSHIP PRINCIPLE 16

When a woman rushes in too quickly, a man will assume she is in love with a "fantasy" or the *idea* of having a relationship. But if he has to slowly win her over, incrementally, he'll think she's falling in love with *who he is.*

RELATIONSHIP PRINCIPLE 17

Don't even mention the word "commitment." ***That's the whole trick.*** **The less you say about it, the closer you are to getting one.**

RELATIONSHIP PRINCIPLE 18

If he has no guarantees, becomes attached, and thinks you could be gone at any time, that's when he'll cherish the idea of securing a relationship.

RELATIONSHIP PRINCIPLE 19

There's nothing more prized to a man than something he had to wait for, work for, or struggle a little bit to get.

RELATIONSHIP PRINCIPLE 20

As soon as a woman hands a man a more serious commitment on a silver platter, he'll be reluctant to take it.

RELATIONSHIP PRINCIPLE 21

Don't be so blunt, obvious, or available that you come across as having already made up your mind about the guy.

RELATIONSHIP PRINCIPLE 22

You want to figure out his pattern, but don't let him figure out yours.

RELATIONSHIP PRINCIPLE 23

Men are far more smitten when they feel like they are "stealing" your time away from something else you could have been doing.

RELATIONSHIP PRINCIPLE 24

When a woman makes a man feel he's trusted, it makes him feel strong and worthy. It makes him want to be honorable and do the right thing.

RELATIONSHIP PRINCIPLE 25

Men like rules and they like guidelines. If there's something you don't like, he'll respect you for voicing it. He wants to know what the "do's and don'ts" are.

RELATIONSHIP PRINCIPLE 26

Men love knowing there's a small part of you that they can't get to.

RELATIONSHIP PRINCIPLE 27

Men read a lot into where you've been, by how dolled up you are when you get home. If you are dolled up and you weren't with him, it will keep him wondering a little.

RELATIONSHIP PRINCIPLE 28

The magic formula is to give a little . . . and then pull back. Give a little . . . and then pull back.

RELATIONSHIP PRINCIPLE 29

Women are constantly being told amazing sex will win a man's heart. This is false. Just because a man sleeps with you doesn't mean he cares about you. Nor will good sex *make him care* about you.

RELATIONSHIP PRINCIPLE 30

The way to weed out the contenders from the pretenders is to assess their attitude about waiting for sex. If he likes you, he'll be happy just being in your company.

RELATIONSHIP PRINCIPLE 31

The purpose of waiting is not just to seem classier. You also want to give yourself time to observe him and find out key facts about him.

RELATIONSHIP PRINCIPLE 32

Who he *tells* you he is in the beginning has very little to do with how he will *treat* you. If there's sex involved, he'll promise you things you've never even heard of.

RELATIONSHIP PRINCIPLE 33

When you aren't mind-blown after sex, and you continue to focus on your own life, he'll automatically start looking at you differently. Then he'll start wanting to secure a relationship with you.

RELATIONSHIP PRINCIPLE 34

After sex, behave as if the relationship is still new.

RELATIONSHIP PRINCIPLE 35

Men are intrigued by anything they do not completely control.

RELATIONSHIP PRINCIPLE 36

When you maintain a bit of privacy and he has to wonder a little where you are, you are stimulating his imagination. The second he can't get ahold of you he'll send out an APB, or "all points bulletin," to find you.

RELATIONSHIP PRINCIPLE 37

To a man, a relationship without sex represents a relationship with no love, no affection, and no emotional connection.

RELATIONSHIP PRINCIPLE 38

Always preserve the mystery. Keep the sex sporadic and unpredictable. It makes it much more intense for a man.

RELATIONSHIP PRINCIPLE 39

When a woman reacts emotionally, men get three things: attention, control, and the feeling of importance.

RELATIONSHIP PRINCIPLE 40

When you are easily manipulated, he will assume he doesn't have to give as much in the way of a commitment in order to keep you there.

RELATIONSHIP PRINCIPLE 41

The best way to set limits with a guy when he's testing you is by controlling the ebb and flow of your attention. An emotional reaction is always a reward, even if it's negative attention.

RELATIONSHIP PRINCIPLE 42

Men *hear* what they *see*.

RELATIONSHIP PRINCIPLE 43

When a man tries to make you jealous, it rarely has anything to do with his desire for someone else. When you are upset he gets the reassurance that you care.

RELATIONSHIP PRINCIPLE 44

Once *you* start doing the same thing *he* was doing, suddenly, the bad behavior will magically disappear.

RELATIONSHIP PRINCIPLE 45

When a man doesn't call, a bunch of scenarios will typically run through a woman's mind. Similarly, his imagination will run wild when he doesn't hear from you.

RELATIONSHIP PRINCIPLE 46

The more rational and calm you remain, the more emotional he will become.

RELATIONSHIP PRINCIPLE 47

To a man, it is totally inappropriate to be emotional when talking about something important. When you speak calmly, he assumes it's much more important.

RELATIONSHIP PRINCIPLE 48

Many men reduce women to a set of givens. A man relies on the fact that most women are emotional and that he'll be able to push your emotional buttons once he finds out where they are. When he can't, he'll often crumble and become the more vulnerable one in the relationship.

RELATIONSHIP PRINCIPLE 49

He is testing to see if you believe in yourself. He wants to know who is at the controls. When you aren't easily shaken he sees, "This one can't be manipulated."

RELATIONSHIP PRINCIPLE 50

To encourage the right behavior, state what you want, and then give him the solution. Show him how he can be your hero.

RELATIONSHIP PRINCIPLE 51

When he's dating you, he'll constantly be on guard and watching to discern, "Does she like me for who I am? Or for what I can provide?"

RELATIONSHIP PRINCIPLE 52

When a man sees you are focused on your own dreams or on elevating yourself, he feels safer marrying you because he doesn't worry about what you'll be trying to take away *from him.*

RELATIONSHIP PRINCIPLE 53

Men don't judge how much money you have. They notice *how you budget* what you do have.

RELATIONSHIP PRINCIPLE 54

Men admire women who want to elevate themselves and pull themselves up by their own bootstraps, and fear women who are social climbers at a man's expense.

RELATIONSHIP PRINCIPLE 55

He doesn't want to marry a helpless little girl whom he will have to take care of.

RELATIONSHIP PRINCIPLE 56

For a man, the words *respect* and *trust* are interchangeable. If he doesn't respect you, he will not trust you. And without trust, he will always keep you at arm's length.

RELATIONSHIP PRINCIPLE 57

When he gives you something, always acknowledge the kindness behind the gesture, not the material item itself. Just like women can't get too many compliments, a man can't get too much appreciation for his contribution.

RELATIONSHIP PRINCIPLE 58

A man's favorite word is *appreciate*. He wants more than anything to feel revered and valued by a woman. When she's appreciative, it motivates him to give her the world.

RELATIONSHIP PRINCIPLE 59

A man will not be thinking about how much he spends on you if he believes you could be "the one." In the beginning, he will be *happy* to pick up the tab.

RELATIONSHIP PRINCIPLE 60

A man who is financially comfortable but still very stingy doesn't want to give—*anything*. He won't to be inconvenienced with his time, with sharing a dresser—much less a home or a life together.

RELATIONSHIP PRINCIPLE 61

When you move into someone else's place, you don't just give up your personal space and belongings. More important, nearly always you also lose your *feeling of independence.*

RELATIONSHIP PRINCIPLE 62

If marriage is extremely important to you and you are ready to set a wedding date, don't move in unless you have a ring and a date.

RELATIONSHIP PRINCIPLE 63

The biggest turn-on for a man is knowing that he is in love with a woman he can really count on, who will *really* be there for him.

RELATIONSHIP PRINCIPLE 64

Set your own timelines and limits, and leave if it's time to get out. Until then, don't let him know about your timelines or deal breakers. Then keep your eyes open and watch how he manages his 50 percent of the relationship. Then you'll get the real deal much quicker.

RELATIONSHIP PRINCIPLE 65

A guy who really thinks you could be "the one" will say very little about marriage. He'll be much more reserved, and will slowly open up over the course of several months, because he won't want to scare you off.

RELATIONSHIP PRINCIPLE 66

The more control you have over yourself, the more of a hold you will have on his heart.

RELATIONSHIP PRINCIPLE 67

If a man really cares, he feels vulnerable. That's when he needs a protective shield the most and that's when he'll often behave more coolly.

RELATIONSHIP PRINCIPLE 68

Whenever boredom sets in, simply break the routine. As soon as the routine changes, it will pique his interest and the relationship will become interesting again.

RELATIONSHIP PRINCIPLE 69

You have a much better chance of getting engaged when a man doesn't feel pressured into it.

RELATIONSHIP PRINCIPLE 70

The bitch won't allow herself to be with a man who is biding his time until something better comes along.

RELATIONSHIP PRINCIPLE 71

The bitch does not hint about marriage or ask, "Where is this going?" Instead, she hints about the removal of herself from the relationship. ***The word*** **marriage** ***never even comes up.***

RELATIONSHIP PRINCIPLE 72

When you stand up for yourself in a dignified, feminine, and womanly way, you can get ***anything*** **you want from a man. When you place a high value on yourself** ***in the right way,*** **so will he.**

RELATIONSHIP PRINCIPLE 73

In life, half the battle has to do with the lens you choose to see yourself through. Your fulfillment hinges on whether you see yourself through a positive lens or a negative one.

RELATIONSHIP PRINCIPLE 74

Men rarely take it as a compliment when you bend over backward or become too agreeable. Men want to feel special, and when you are *too nice* he feels ordinary, because he assumes you'd acquiesce and become a yes-person with *any man*.

RELATIONSHIP PRINCIPLE 75

He doesn't marry a woman who puts him on a throne. He marries a woman who is his equal . . . that special woman whom he can share all of life's special moments with.

INDEX

A

B

P

R

S